The Virtual Ticket

How to Host Private Live Streams
& Virtual Events

By Paul William Richards

ISBN: 9798625066358

DEDICATION

This book is dedicated to the team who helped host the 2019 StreamGeeks Summit. You know who you are.

Online Course Available Here:
https://www.udemy.com/course/virtual-tickets

Facebook User Group -
https://www.facebook.com/groups/TheVirtualTicket

CONTENTS

ACKNOWLEDGMENTS

I'd like to acknowledge Bill Mullin as a mentor. Bill's deep thinking is contagious and sometimes brilliant. Thank you for all the amazing book recommendations that helped to influence the *The Virtual Ticket*.

1 THE EVENTS INDUSTRY: RIPE FOR A REBRAND

How many trillion-dollar industries are expected to double in size over the next ten years? The $1.1 trillion dollar global event industry is expected to grow to $2.33 trillion by 2026, (Allied Market Research, 2019). Analysts have been astounded by the growth in the events industry over the past decade. A new "experience economy" has been coined to describe the changing consumer behaviors which have emerged during the age of the smartphone. Despite the incredible amounts of screen time modern consumers spend on their smartphones, computers and other internet-connected devices, humans still crave exciting in-real-life experiences.

The instantaneous access modern consumers have to information has significantly changed the way consumers value exclusive content. The endless streams of entertainment available today have made consumers more willing than ever to pay for all kinds of premium content that enhances time spent on and offline. Today consumers want to break through the clutter of a technology saturated life with shortcuts that could be as simple as unlocking a premium video or as dynamic as paying for a virtual VIP video conference with a popular celebrity. As event managers begin to understand this culture shift, they can position the experiences they offer to global audiences with exclusive virtual tickets that have an unlimited supply.

Great events start by understanding an audience. Event managers who understand their audience can deliver an experience that both excites and engages. Unlike traditional business services which are all about *time well saved*, experiences worth paying for are about *time well spent* (Pine, 2020). Today more than ever, audiences are willing to pay to make more of their time "well spent" and therefore less of their time searching for satisfaction. If your event provides consumers with a feeling of time well spent, you have an experience worthy of delivering value virtually. In the #1 selling book "The Experience Economy" authors Joseph Pine and James Gilmore explain why "Time is the currency of experiences" and increasing brand exposure via consumer attention now requires the ability to deliver an engaging experience. Event experiences are unique because they unfold in real-time. Exclusive virtual access to an event can deliver audiences a real-time experience. At the core of these authentic experiences is **time**. Live streaming technology can deliver experiences in real-time. Connections that are made in real-time, are the as close to real for the viewers as they are for audiences attending the event in-person.

Value Experience Diagram

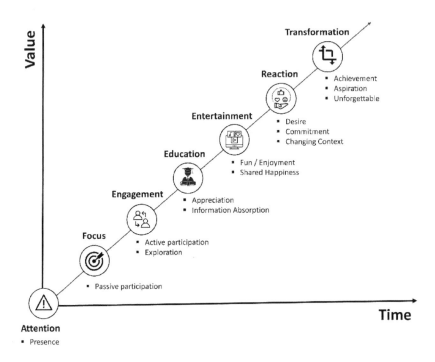

Well-designed events can easily transport viewers into an immersive experience using live streaming technology. There is an immediacy created with live streaming that is authentic and real in a world of fragmented media. Facebook released a report saying that live video is watched on average three times longer than traditional video content (Facebook, 2017). This is because live video creates a real-time connection with viewers that captivates their attention. Although attention is only the first step toward an ultimate goal of transformation. When presented corrected, attention can lead to focus, which can lead to engagement, education, reaction and transformation. Viewers that participate with the live action, can experience authentic connections and revelations with an online community in real-time.

But how can you create an experience that engages audiences? How can you capture the audience's attention and leave them with a cliffhanger worth the $50 virtual ticket fee? Live broadcasting events is not a new concept. It's well known that live broadcasts can sustain an event's essential elements to move people. Just look at New York City's New Year's Eve Ball Drop Ceremony, which has been broadcast on live television since the 1940s. The difference today is that broadcast technology is affordable for any business to use. The internet infrastructure available to reach consumers is widespread and the devices used to connect with this type of media is commonplace. Consumers today value experiences over products and convenience is more important than cost, in many cases.

From a basic economic perspective, virtual ticket sales are a simple way for event planners to extend their audience and thereby increase profitability. But this book won't stop at profitability. This book was written to encourage event planners to push the limits of their creativity and apply new technologies to broadcast these ideas to large online audiences (Pine, 2020).

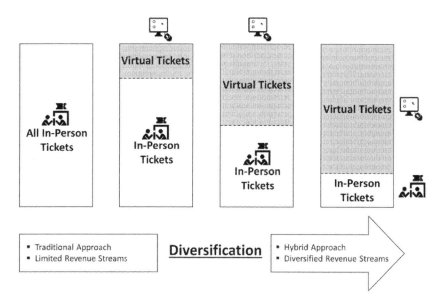

Adding virtual tickets to your event will increase revenue diversification. The process of revenue diversification can become a crucial part of any event's growth development strategy. The traditional approach to events can be transformed into a hybrid approach that increases market penetration opportunities. As the events industry becomes more diversified by increasing attendance options, it will also become less vulnerable to external forces. The recent global coronavirus outbreak has abruptly reminded the events industry how quickly outside forces can threaten event success. For example, South by Southwest, a major music and technology festival expected to draw 100,000 attendees in March 2020, was cancelled due to the coronavirus outbreaks. In extreme cases like this, a virtual ticket option can serve as a backup plan for cancelled events that are out of the event planner's control.

Events can be further diversified with virtual ticket sales by offering broadcast options in new languages. In an upcoming chapter, you will learn how to easily set up broadcasts that support live-transcription options in hundreds of different languages. Technology today can easily allow event managers to broadcast tape-delayed live streams which include live audio translations for simultaneous broadcasts to audiences who speak different languages. The diagram below shows a LAN (local area network) that can be set up to broadcast a main broadcast to multiple sources with live translators. The technology used to produce broadcast translations has come down in price dramatically.

Live Broadcast Translation

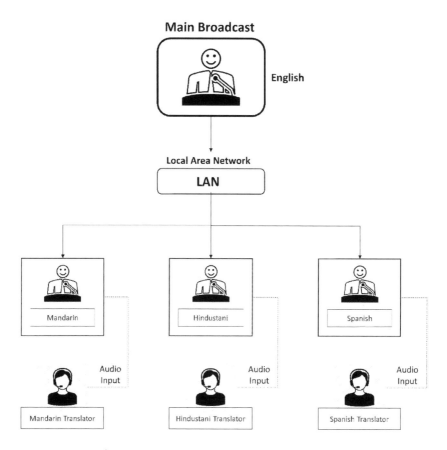

Music concerts, festivals, sports, conferences, and corporate events are all predicted to grow significantly throughout the next decade. In a technology saturated world, live events are cutting through the clutter and delivering consumers the type of valued experiences they are willing to spend their hard-earned money on. One study, "Cashing in on the U.S experience economy" by McKinsey & Company, reports that experience spending has increased 6.7% between 2014 to 2016. The market for spectator sports has increased by a stunning 10% over the same period. The music industry, for example, has gone through many changes of the past decade. Live artist performances and tours have helped revive profits for the industry during a time when widespread illegal content distribution threatened the industry's growth. A drastic drop in album sales has caused artists to rethink their fan experience strategy and focus on creating memorable events that amaze live audiences. Further opportunities for growth in the music industry will allow artists to connect with fans using live streaming while on tour (Pine, 2020).

With all this growth and renewal in the events industry, the potential for virtual ticket sales is remains a largely untapped opportunity. For many event managers, visualizing what the process will look like for their specific event remains a challenge. In many cases, event managers aim to "control and manage" in order to maximize event success. For event managers, this can become a process of eliminating the opportunity for something to go wrong. Attempting to manage the expectations of event goers on site often leaves the online audience as an afterthought. Event managers may be asking themselves, who is this online audience? How can you create an experience for people watching online? What type of experience are they expecting? How does an event planner manage the expectations of a live audience they can't see? Event managers who lack an appropriate strategy often neglect to address the virtual ticket opportunity because they have too many other pressing matters to attend to before the event's deadline.

The good news is that you have this book. It's a new decade, and there are plenty of virtual ticket success stories you can learn from in order to implement your own immersive live streaming experience. After all, great events are celebrations. How many times have you watched the New Year's Eve Ball Drop on TV? Has it ever made you feel the urge to kiss someone? Have you felt the energy beaming out of the television at midnight? This is the type of energy that the best live broadcasts can capture and transmit over the internet.

Connecting to an online audience can help event planner better accomplish core event goals. When implemented correctly, virtual tickets should not have a negative impact on the established revenue generation model. The issue for most event managers is the uncertainty. Selling virtual tickets introduces an array of possible issues that busy event managers have little experience managing. That is why this book seeks to outline the benefits of event streaming and set the stage for hosting impactful online experiences consumers are willing to pay for. You will learn about new tools that not only simplify the process of live streaming but also how to make the experience more manageable. In this way, you will have the opportunity to study strategies for marketing your own virtual experience and uncover new ways of explaining the value to your customers. Starting from the pre-planning stages of your event, this book will walk you through the essential steps toward creating an amazing online virtual ticket experience that can complement any event. So, get ready. It's time to plan out some of the most powerful and under-utilized revenue opportunities for event planning today.

2 RIP OFF THE BAND-AID AND SELL THOSE VIRTUAL TICKETS

The year is 2017, and it's a hazy day in Los Angeles, California. Top YouTuber Derral Eves is working with his team to host the 4th annual Vidsummit conference. Vidsummit is a highly anticipated video marketing event, where the world's top influencers, marketers and brands get together each year for a weekend of learning and networking. This year Gary Vaynerchuk has been hired to provide the keynote speech, and Derral is planning to sell virtual tickets for the first time. After three successful annual events, Derral is confident that this year he can increase profits with virtual ticket sales. The event is already sold out. There is an incredible buzz on social media and the countdown until showtime has officially begun.

The Westin Los Angeles Airport Hotel is absolutely packed with young YouTubers from all over the world. Video enthusiasts are filming videos in the lobby and making memories with friends. In the main ballroom, Derral has agreed to make time for a brief interview. "You can only fit so many people in a room" Derral says as he looks over the 500 or so chairs setup in the ballroom. "We knew that we had to extend this conference online... We have sold replays in the past and it has been quite profitable. But the problem is getting the excitement delivered to the customer with a live event like this. We want people to feel like they are actually part of the event." Derral looks over the shoulders of a staff member who oversees social media. His social media team will be live streaming certain portions of the conference to his YouTube channel which has well over half a million subscribers. Part of the virtual ticket sales strategy is live streaming short sessions throughout the conference to YouTube and Facebook. Derral's team is preparing a live streaming backpack which will be used to transport audiences behind the scenes to various areas of the conference.

In total, the event features three live streaming systems used to capture content from the main ballroom, a 125-seat theater and a large meeting space. Each space will be running a separate track of speakers, giving attendees plenty of educational opportunities to choose from throughout the three-day event. A normal ticket to the conference costs $795 and any attendee can purchase access to the video replay and live stream for an additional $149. Now that the in-person tickets have sold out, the conference is only able to sell virtual tickets and on-demand replays.

It was my job to help transport the live viewers into VidSummit. I would do so by delivering the live stream to a content delivery network who in turn provides the paywall service used to grant access to paying customers. This is a process you will learn all about in this book.

Before the conference had even begun, excited virtual ticket holders were actively commenting about the event on Facebook. Many of these people sounded just as excited to be part of VidSummit's live stream as the actual in-person attendees at the hotel. Along with the live stream access, most attendees had also paid for the on-demand video access knowing that they couldn't possibly watch every presentation in real time. The live stream was an exciting bonus Derral had announced only a couple of weeks ago.

Customer Virtual Ticket Process

Customer Buys Virtual Ticket	**Customer Gains Virtual Login**	**Customer Watches Live Stream**

• Through Your Website • Through Affiliated Website	• Via Text or Email • Unique Login Credentials	• Available on Mac, PC and Smartphones

In this book, you will learn how to build amazing virtual experiences that online viewers will happily pay for. Over my years in the live streaming industry, I have seen the best and the worst of online pay-per-view. The very first pay-per-view event happened in 1948 when a boxing match was broadcast to a select group of theaters and viewing venues in black and white. Today over seventy years later, pay-per-view streaming technology is 100% scalable and surprisingly affordable for the everyday business. By reading this book and taking the online course you will learn how to market and produce cutting edge live streams that can become a significant source of revenue for your event. This book is designed for event planners and entrepreneurs who want to get their live stream right the first time and save face before messing up a big event. But before you dig into planning a pay-per-view event, check out the interview with Derral Eves about his first experience monetizing a live stream at VidSummit.

An interview with Derral Eves

Is this the first year VidSummit has live streamed the conference?

"Yes, this is the first year we have been able to live stream the event. The thing that we have been doing is trying to get this message out to more people. We can only fit so many people in one room, and we knew we had to do this online. We have sold replay in the past and we have actually been quite profitable with that, but the problem is building the excitement. We wanted to share the excitement of the live event with our online viewers and that is why we went with the Virtual Ticket."

How important are Virtual Ticket sales to the conference?

"Virtual Tickets can make any conference more profitable, because there is fixed overhead and you don't have to worry about the traditional expenses such as hotel fees. All you have to worry about is having the right equipment with the right partners."

What is the percentage of conference attendee's vs virtual attendees? How many additional conference attendees were added because of the Virtual Tickets?

"People at home are able to watch the event in their pajamas. Our viewers are interacting in the chat room online and they are seeing the event from all around the world. Along with the live viewers, the video on-demand is a very big deal for us after the conference. The virtual ticket holders get the choice to choose which talks they want to tune into and with the on-demand access everyone has the ability to go back and watch talks that they missed. In fact, 98% of our virtual ticket holders also purchased the on-demand access ($49 upcharge)."

Were you at all worried about virtual ticket sales undermining the value of in-person ticket sales?

"We had some people who could not make it and they bought the virtual tickets. There is always more happening at the event that you will never get from a virtual ticket. The discussions outside and relationships that are forged you cannot get from a virtual ticket. The only thing I wish we would have done is offer the virtual tickets from day 1. We started selling the tickets a little late and could have capitalized on even more sales."

What tips do you have for others selling virtual tickets at an event?

"We knew we would have a lot of people looking for where to go to watch the live event with their virtual tickets. So, we put a button right on the home page prompting more sales through the event and directing ticket holders to the correct place to watch the live event. We sold another 100 right after we put a promotion stream on my social media accounts. It's probably even more than 100 because my phone is off the hook with emails and sales confirmation right now."

Derral seemed excited after the interview which was later posted to YouTube. Derral did not disclose exactly how much money his conference made from the virtual ticket sales partially because that number was still growing during the interview. The additional virtual ticket sales apparently "covered the costs" for the event which had to be about $100-250k.

After watching how profitable virtual ticket sales were for Derral in 2017, I went in search of more opportunities like this. I was so inspired that our team at StreamGeeks eventually ended up starting our own Summit two years later called the "StreamGeeks Summit." This case study will share exactly how much money was made and how important virtual ticket sales can be.

About six months after the StreamGeeks Summit, I realized how much more affordable it would be to host a 100% online summit. This idea led to another event we hosted called the "Worship Summit Live." This event was designed to cater to the online audience with a focus on education. Virtual ticket sales have quickly become an important part of the communications efforts at our company.

Using these experiences as a guide, I realized that hosting events is an amazing opportunity for companies small and large. The next few chapters of this book will review some of the basics surrounding the art of event planning. From a planning perspective, this book will uncover valuable opportunities for event managers who want to include a virtual audience in their event. You will of course learn how to sell virtual tickets and hopefully benefit from multiple case studies and business models that are examined for virtual event monetization.

3 THE CASE STUDIES

Case Study #1 – NAB Show

Every year the StreamGeeks travel to many conferences around the world. In most cases, the events do not offer virtual ticket experiences. It seems like most conferences are unprepared to address an online audience. In 2019, the StreamGeeks team was invited to help host the official NAB (National Association of Broadcasters) Show live stream, in Las Vegas, Nevada. If there is one organization that knows how to live stream, you can bet it's the National Association of Broadcasters. The experience of hosting a television quality show was thrilling not only because of the size and scope of the production but because of the large in-person audience. Imagine a voice in your ear counting down the seconds until you go live. Lights are shining on the stage from every direction, "3, 2, 1, And we are live."

This type of production value is ideal for large conferences with thousands of attendees. It may be surprising for some to find out that the NAB Show does not charge viewers for access to the live stream. The production is put on mainly for sponsors allowing the show to sell additional advertising. It may also be surprising to find out that the show is not live streamed to Facebook. The NAB Show values control of their content more than the exposure they would gain via social media. When you start to dig into the various case studies available for adding live streaming to an event, the possibilities for customization are almost limitless. Sadly, the 2020 NAB show was cancelled due to the coronavirus outbreak. This year the live stream is scheduled to be recorded and live streamed from a remote location to viewers around the world.

This book will reference quite a few case studies throughout. These unique experiences have been thoughtfully planned out and studied for the creation of this book. The first is the NAB show, which is the world's largest broadcast and streaming show. The second is a well-established conference called VidSummit designed for video makers. This case study which helped to introduce the book, explores strategies event managers can use to increase profits with live streaming and on-demand virtual ticket sales. The third case study is the 2019 StreamGeeks Summit, which was hosted in New York City to provide a full day of live streaming education. This event was the StreamGeeks best attempt to give online attendees virtual access to a small conference. Finally, the fourth case study is the 2020 Worship Summit. This event was designed with the online attendees as the primary focus. This event could be categorized as a "digital summit" or a glorified webinar where meeting the online attendees' expectations was the primary goal of the event planner.

Case Study #2 - VidSummit

Check out the event page here: https://vidsummit.com

VidSummit has been ahead of the curve since 2015 when they started selling on-demand videos that were made available to paying customers. In 2017, Derral Eves launched his first year of virtual ticket sales with live event access. The conference live stream included access to a keynote speech area and multiple breakout rooms running three separate presentation tracks. Each room was set up to live stream the content simultaneously giving online viewers the option to virtually switch between rooms and drop in on various presentations in real time. Being able to live stream from multiple areas is a process that medium to large events will need to develop in order to cover their events properly. Online audiences understand that they will not have access to all things at all times. Derral Eves was able to use social media to promote virtual ticket sales with high-impact IRL (In Real Life) streaming techniques that leverage a LiveU backpack and a mobile Sony action camera. You will also learn how Eves empowers other creators to sell tickets using an affiliate program. Finally, this case study will demonstrate how a conference can add a virtual ticket experience to an existing event.

Case Study #3 - The StreamGeeks Summit
Check out the event page here: http://streamgeeks.us/summit

The next case study explained in this book is the first annual StreamGeeks Summit. This conference was designed to provide a "full day of live streaming education" in New York City. The conference brought together a growing community of video production enthusiasts from the NYC area and created common ground for novices and experts in the industry to intermingle. The conference also served as a case study for integrating a professional live stream into a traditional in-person conference.

Roughly 900 tickets were sold for the StreamGeeks Summit. Only 250 of those tickets were sold for in-person attendance. The in-person tickets sold for $295 each. The other 650 tickets were a mix of basic and premium virtual ticket sales. Basic virtual tickets for the event were completely free with the submission of a form. Premium virtual tickets were sold for $95 each and they were included for free with in-person passes. In this case study, over 250% more virtual tickets were sold than in-person tickets. Established events will likely see a steady increase in virtual ticket sales after the first year assuming the experience is marketed and delivered successfully.

Newly established events like the StreamGeeks Summit can leverage free virtual tickets in the first few years to help drive increased ticket sales via exposure over the long term. Using the basic virtual tickets to draw in new potential ticket buyers, this case study will shed light on virtual ticket sales, premium on-demand sales, and their effect on planning the event overall.

Case Study #4 - The Worship Summit
Check out the event page here: https://worshipsummit.live

The final case study will review the 2020 Worship Summit hosted by the StreamGeeks in West Chester, Pennsylvania. This event included a hybrid meetup style event where most attendees joined online. This was a small-scale event in terms of in-person ticket sales, with only 30 in-person attendees. But on Friday morning, January 24th, 2020, the event was one of the top live streams on YouTube with almost 400 simultaneous viewers at peak viewership. Before the event was over more than 5,000 churches had tuned in.

Case Study: 2020 Worship Summit

While the event featured an in-person studio experience, most guests joined remotely. This event also included a live face-to-face zoom video conference breakout session for attendees. The video conference meeting was open during the entire event and it allowed attendees to get more personal with the event speakers who would join for 30-45 minutes after their main stage presentation. This event falls in line with a new trend called "Virtual Summits." Virtual summit are events where experts get together to produce an engaging online experience for viewers around the world.

4 HIGH LEVEL: HOW DO I SELL VIRTUAL TICKETS

Virtual tickets can be sold through almost any event ticketing platform. As an event planner, you know the value of a ticket sold is only as good as the event that you host and deliver. In order to deliver a live event experience to online viewers, you must live stream your event in a way that engages viewers' senses. Today, you can live stream directly from a smartphone to social media networks like Facebook and YouTube. Depending on the ticket price and the value you are attempting to deliver, properly transporting audiences into your event may take an experienced video production team and a thoughtful plan of delivery.

Virtual ticket holder expectations will continue to rise over time. Consumers value the experience of "time well spent" in relation to other experiences they consider normal. The Experience Economy calls this valuation the "money value of time," which is generally broken down into dollars per minute. For example, most consumers in the United States are used to paying on average $12 for a two-hour experience at the movies. This is a simple baseline for how much consumers are willing to pay for an action-packed Hollywood experience. At $6 per hour, moviegoers are paying on average 10 cents per minute. This experience can be compared to a trip to Disney World which averages out to 23 cents per minute for a vacation. Here is a list of experiences your event may be able to compare with.

Experience	Money Value of Time*
Trip to the Movies	10 cents per minute
Trip to Disney World	23 cents per minute
Round of Golf at Pebble Beach	$2 per minute
iFly Skydiving Simulator	$43 per minute
Skydiving Experience	$200 per minute
Trip to outer space	$1,750 per minute

*Price estimates from The Experience Economy. (Pine, 2020).

A careful consideration of the value you are attempting to deliver will help you determine a price for your virtual tickets. Once you have determined the price, you can start planning your live stream much like the event itself. Now it's time to consider the high-level workflow for delivering your event to an online audience. A paywall is a service provided by a premium CDN (content delivery network) that manages who can gain access to your private live stream. If you have paying customers, you only want those customers to be able to access the premium experience that they have paid for. This is what the paywall service does for you by managing your list of paying customers and gating access for attendees who still need to purchase tickets.

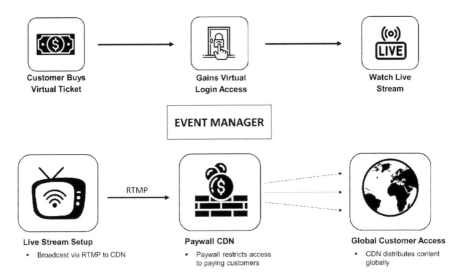

Paywalls are becoming more and more commonplace as the internet has become a global marketplace for premium digital content. Influencers have become one of the most successful groups online to take advantage of paywalls. There are many ways to monetize access to your premium content and watching the trends set by online Instagram influencers' may actually garner interesting business strategies for the modern event planner. Vogue Business writer Kati Chitrakorn recently studied influencer's use of paywalls writing "Influencers with big followings on Instagram and other platforms are starting to put up 'paywalls' by charging fans for exclusive content. Some charge a monthly fee to become a 'Close Friend' on Instagram, while others are trialing WeChat's new paywalls. In effect, content quality is becoming a focus. While these payments add another revenue stream for influencers, analysts say brand partnerships will remain as a source of credibility" (VogueBusiness, 2020). Supporting an Instagram influencer may be a good experience for you if you are planning on selling virtual tickets.

It's an easy way to put yourself in the shoes of the buyer and see if you get any value from the Instagram influencer of your choice.

Over 100,000 influencers worldwide are currently using a platform called Patreon which offers tiered premium content subscriptions for fans. Since it's start, Patreon has paid out over $1 billion dollars to creators such as musicians, podcasters, visual artists, writers, gamers, non-profits, and educators. Patreon offers a subscription model which provides customers access to premium content. Consider searching through Patreon and finding a creator that sparks your interest. You can commit to supporting a creator starting at only $1 per month. Using Patreon you can see the type of value you get from a paid digital relationship. Try it out and see if the creator reaches out to you directly. Learn how the platform works and start to understand the engagement and connections these virtual commitments can inspire (Patreon, 2020).

After supporting your first Patreon, it's time to head over to Vimeo to see how professional video creators are monetizing their content. Vimeo is very much like a professional version of YouTube. With a professional Vimeo account, you can sell, rent, and offer subscriptions to your videos starting at just $20/month. Vimeo does take 10% of the revenue, but that is a small price to pay for a service like this. Vimeo also allows event managers the ability to launch their own streaming service. The Vimeo streaming service includes an option to have a custom branded app for your event starting at only $500 (as of March 2020). An app like this can be downloaded by virtual attendees around the world giving them a premium experience for viewing your event.

Later, in the book, you will see comparisons between Vimeo and other premium live streaming services. For now, familiarize yourself with the way premium content creators are marketing and selling their videos online. Try purchasing a premium video. Experience the process and imagine a list of videos from your next event hosted online in this way. How many videos would you have? How much would you charge? The 2019 StreamGeeks Summit hosted on-demand videos on an online education site called Udemy. While you have less control over your content on Udemy, it was a better fit for that project. If your event is about education, consider an online learning site like Udemy which has an engaged online audience looking for educational content. Vimeo is great for all types of content, and it has an easy upgrade path for live streaming as well.

Now it's time to join a private Facebook group. Starting in 2019, Facebook has been marketing its groups feature to bring together like-minded individuals on the platform. You can start by looking for groups that may be interested in your event. Or you could perhaps choose a group dedicated to a personal interest or hobby of your own. The point of this exercise is to learn how niche online group communities form and interact. Notice how the group moderators lay down the rules and maintain order. See how the dedicated group news feed allows you to find specific group content. Perhaps most importantly, see how quickly information from the group starts to spread into your organic Facebook newsfeed.

Now you might be thinking, what does a private Facebook group have to do with selling virtual tickets? First, Facebook groups are an amazing social experiment that can help you understand how online communities work. When you host an exclusive live stream for a group of people online, your goal should be to create an engaging experience for individuals and the community. One of the most important parts of the online experience is the community that participates with the event live in the moment. Online communities today can be very strong and close-knit. When social media works best, people can forge new relationships that span the globe and make them feel more connected. If you want to understand online community building, there is no substitute for joining an online community and making friends online. Start by commenting on something that is interesting to you. Perhaps you would like to share an article you read online or a silly comment about your day. Just like real in-person relationships, it will take time to learn the names of people you relate to. Many online communities are groups of friends, co-workers, and peers who meet up only occasionally. For the rest of the year, members of online communities can stay in contact online maintaining relationships that may have otherwise faded away.

Starting your own Facebook group could serve as an extension for your event where relationships can continue to grow online. Did you know that you can live stream directly to a Facebook group? Some savvy Facebook group moderators will have a large group for a specific topic and a premium paid group for their subscribers. Some influencers will even use services like Patreon as their paywall and only allow paying subscribers into their premium Facebook group. In this way, you can create a paywall system that includes 100% free live streaming to group members. Most premium paywalls charge event planners for the bandwidth used by viewers. Depending on your service provider, the free Facebook option could save your event thousands of dollars in streaming fees. In any case, your premium group members will gain a community group area where in-person and online virtual ticket holders can network after your event. Once the event is over, you can start a new group for the next version of your event keeping the old group in place for networking purposes. In this way, you can create alumni style groups of people who have all shared an experience virtually or in-person at your event.

Regardless of how you decide to set up your virtual ticket sales and content delivery, your focus should be on managing expectations. That is why this book has a focus on the planning of your virtual ticket sales and strategies for delivering the highest value virtual experiences. When it comes to delivering high-value live engaging content, you don't have to go too far to find examples. Look for influencers in your space, be it corporate, entertainment, music, or training. Yes, you need to deliver an amazing experience in order to charge for virtual tickets. But the online tools surrounding social media, event planning, video production, and live streaming are at your disposal to create revenue streams that can take your event to new heights.

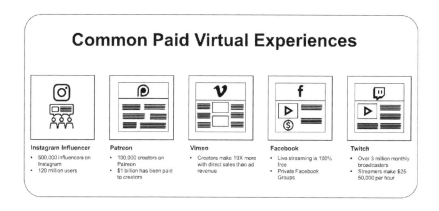

The good news is that you are already planning an event and much of the excitement driving marketing work is already generating the buzz you need to cultivate virtual ticket demand. Promoting an event is nothing new for event managers. What is new is translating the best parts of the event into an online experience. This takes you to the final social media experiment you need to partake in before planning a virtual ticket experience. It's time to check out Twitch.tv. Even if you aren't a big fan of online video gaming, it's worth watching some live streams on Twitch. Twitch is the leading online live streaming website for gamers. Millions of viewers tune in everyday to watch their favorite creators and engage with the online communities that they are a part of. This is where you can purchase your first set of virtual currency that you can use to pay creators. Twitch calls its virtual currency "bits" and they can be used to effectively tip creators for their content.

Start by searching through Twitch and finding a creator you think is interesting. Once you have logged in you can join a chat room and engage in a unique live stream experience. When you feel compelled, take out your wallet and buy $10 worth of bits (1,000 bits). Depending on how impressed you are with the content, type in your custom message into the chatroom and include a couple hundred bits. Think about what you just did. You just bought a virtual experience. You just paid for the experience of virtually tipping a content creator and possibly getting live recognition for your contribution. Hopefully the creator will respond in real-time thanking you for the donation. Take note of how this experience makes you feel. Simply being recognized by someone else in real-time in front of of an audience. Now you are starting to understand the power of live streaming and audience engagement. You can learn a lot about live viewer engagement from Twitch streamers. There are thousands of streamers on Twitch who make a living through a mixture of paid subscribers and online donations. The more interactive and engaging the live content is, the more money these Twitch streamers will generally make.

Congratulations. You have now supported an Instagram influencer, become a Patreon, joined a private Facebook group and dropped some virtual bits into a Twitch stream. Let these experiences start to sink in as you plan out the virtual ticket experience for your next event. Continue to have new experiences with online communities and focus on the moments that you feel most engaged and entertained. This is the feeling you will be striving to recreate with your next virtual ticket experience.

5 EVENT PLANNING AND MANAGEMENT

If you have ever attended an event that was professionally planned and executed, chances are you didn't realize how much work went into making it a success. Events, regardless of their size, are complex things to manage. In every event, something goes wrong, and if you are lucky the only people who notice are on the event management team. An issue can be something minor like forgetting to bring the right color socks, or a major catastrophe, like leaving the wedding ring behind at the hotel. Whatever it is, events and uncertainty go together like two peas in a pod. This may be why so many amazing events are unable to add a live streaming element. It's very common for event planners to become overwhelmed and unable to add another layer of complexity that is live streaming. Selling virtual tickets is one thing, accommodating a live online audience is another.

Therefore, whether you are a professional event manager or a one-time event planner, having a framework that introduces order into the messy process of event-planning is crucial. A systematic approach allows you to deliver excellent results even when you do not have the help of a professional event planning team. An event planning system saves cost, reduces work, removes uncertainty, and makes your success repeatable.

Event management software solutions can give multiple teams in your organization access to critical information during the event planning process. Having a single online dashboard for sales, marketing, human resources, sponsors and affiliates helps to simplify the complex job of event planning. New cloud-based tools now allow event managers to streamline an efficient workflow that keeps internal and external parties involved in the planning process. Effectively streamlining an event management workflow requires integration with existing systems your organization already uses such as Salesforce, Marketo, Eventbrite, Wordpress and Cvent. When you are choosing an event management platform, draw out a plan that starts with the promotion of your event. It's ideal if your event management software makes relevant information readily available to all members of your team and at the same time passes the data to the primary systems your organization already uses. For example, your event management software should be able to pass usable data directly to your sales team for immediate follow up. If your marketing team is using a platform like Marketo to nurture new leads, the information collected by the event management system should pass back and forth naturally. In this way, you can make intelligent decisions about how you are communicating with your event attendees. Perhaps you only want to offer attendees who have purchased virtual tickets a discount for in-person tickets or vice versa. With the right amount of information passing through your streamlined workflow, sales and marketing teams especially can make educated decisions about your event.

In this book, you will learn the basics of applying a project management approach to event planning in order to properly add a virtual attendee experience to your event. A project is typically described as an endeavor that is temporary and undertaken with specific objectives in mind. Projects have a time element and they require resources in order to produce the desired outcome. Managing a virtual attendee experience will leverage similar types of knowledge, skills, and tools event planners are used to managing already. The goal of event planning is to remove or reduce uncertainty and to make sure the event is executed on schedule, within budgets and on target for intended goals ("What is project management?," 2017).

By applying project management knowledge and skills to event planning, you can more easily add live streaming and virtual ticket sales to your event. Even if you do not consider yourself an event planner, this book can still help you learn about new ways to monetize events. Almost every profession involves events at some point and this book will teach you how to successfully plan and execute them. The "Experience Economy" is a #1 bestselling book that outlines how changing consumer demands now require any competitive business to create experiences for their customers. All businesses are now "competing for customer time, attention and money" where the ROI (Return on Investment) of traditional marketing methods continue to become less valuable. By understanding both the in-person and online sides of meetups, summits, concerts and conferences you will start to see the advantages of event streaming for marketing any type of business product, service or experience. If you are only thinking about the people who can attend your event physically, it will become clear in short order that this audience is only a small segment of the total accessible market. In the following chapters, you will learn how to identify and market your event to online audiences around the world. Depending on your event, the online audience may surprise you in its size and willingness to pay for virtual access (Pine, 2020).

6 DESIGNING A VIRTUAL TICKET EXPERIENCE

A virtual ticket should allow customers the ability to seamlessly access your event from anywhere with internet. Whether your customers use an app or a website connection, they will be able to view the event's live stream with the click of a button. This, of course, means that your event has a live streaming system in place. Secondly, it means you have a system in place for accepting payments and granting access to your exclusive live stream. There are three ways that you can hold your event

- *The Traditional Way*: The event is held at a brick-and-mortar location (hotel, concert hall, etc) and people must be physically present at the venue to be part of the event.

- *The Virtual Event*: The event is completely online. 100% virtual events have no physical venue. These events are live streamed in a studio or other location and people view the sessions online.

- *The Hybrid Event*: A mix of traditional and virtual. Although the event is held at a physical location, people can participate remotely by logging into the online stream.

The hybrid model is perhaps the most attractive way to sell virtual tickets. Along with selling "real tickets" for physical access to your event venue, you can also sell "virtual tickets" to viewers who wish they could attend in person but cannot for one reason or another. The convenience of virtual tickets is a major selling point for many customers. Making virtual attendance so convenient, you may wonder if this will affect the sales of in-person attendance at the event. This section of the guide will help you examine the issues and consider various approaches to set up your event for virtual ticketing ("Want to Monetize your live stream at your next event? - StreamGeeks," n.d.).

Virtual Ticketing: Common Fears & Objections
#1: Virtual tickets will distract attention from the offline event

#2: Virtual tickets will reduce sales of in-person tickets and affect event attendance

Many event organizers fear that offering virtual tickets for an event will cannibalize the in-person event by negatively impacting sales and devaluing the importance of physically attending the event. Although these are valid concerns, they do not necessarily have to be true for your event.

Why People Attend Events

The primary motives that drive people to attend an in-person event involve the experiences that they can obtain from the physical event. Great event planners know how to stimulate the five human senses (sight, touch, smell, hearing, and taste) to create unforgettable experiences. The marketing of your event should make clear distinctions between the in-person experience and the virtual experience. By making the cost of the in-person tickets more expensive than virtual tickets, you are implying that the in-person experience is the most valuable option.

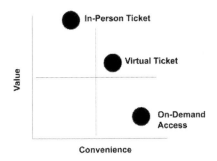

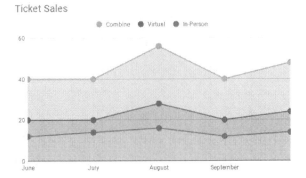

Virtual tickets are usually less expensive and therefore not as valuable in buyers' minds. A primary motivation for virtual ticket buyers is the convenience of experience delivery. On the other hand, the lack of convenience may be a primary objection for many serious buyers who want to attend your event. In this way, virtual tickets allow your event to capture more buyers with busy schedules who are unable to attend in person. While virtual tickets are usually less expensive, that doesn't mean that you can't make more money selling virtual tickets than in-person tickets. A healthy event should have a diversified customer base which includes in-person and virtual ticket holders. While many people like to attend events in person, it's easier for repeat customers to watch from home. Some customers may only pay the premium required for the in-person tickets once, if the event does not offer a significantly new experience each time the event is held. It may be possible to extend the lifespan of customers who want to relive your event in a new way from home with a virtual ticket. If your event is sold out virtual tickets allow you to continue to capture paying customers passed the point of full venue occupancy. If your event is a success you will be happy to have an event option with unlimited capacity ("Why Do People Attend Events? | Meetings Imagined," n.d.).

Designing Your Experience

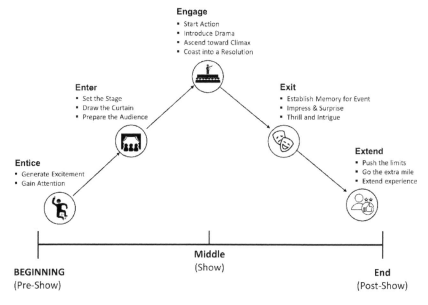

When designing your experience, you should have both in-person and virtual attendees in mind. Virtual ticket viewers are watching an event unfold through a screen. From an event management perspective, it's easier to have absolute control over the broadcast. A cohesive experience should have a clear beginning, middle and end. The diagram above outlines some of the key experience stages you should plan to take your online audience through. You can start by enticing your audience and exciting their imagination about what is to come next. This can be done with announcers the way that sports games are hyped up, or with behind the scenes tours of exclusive areas of your event. When your production enters the main scene there should be a clear start that your audience is prepared for.

In-Person	Virtual
• Sight	• Sight
• Hearing	• Hearing
• Touch	• N/A
• Taste	• N/A
• Smell	• N/A

As the event starts you should attempt to engage your audience. With a virtual audience you must rely on sight and sound to prompt engagement. During the engagement stage you are trying to encourage both passive and active engagement. As viewers are actively responding to what is going on, you can use education and entertainment to re-enforce the most valuable parts of your event. The best events have memorable moments. A great event should always have a planned climax. Transporting the online audience into this climactic experience can be done in many ways. Mobile roving cameras for example, can be used to transport the audience into a first-person point of view inside the event. While this type of view has its limitations, it's a great way to capture exciting high energy moments. One of the most memorable moments of an event can be the exit. Your goal should be to thrill and intrigue your audience, leaving them wanting more. From here, you can extend the experience with behind the scenes interviews and exclusive access.

Value Experience Diagram

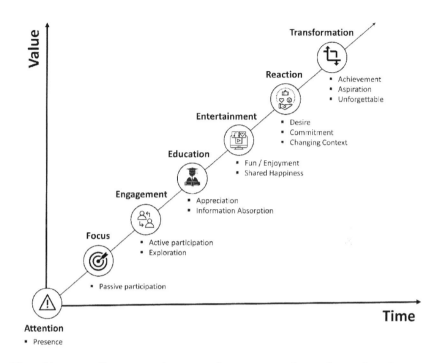

The ultimate audience reaction provokes a personal transformation. In order to provoke a transformation, your audience will have to commit their attention and focus through a process of engagement. Many events use a combination of education or entertainment, popularly referred to as "edutainment." Edutainment is a process of learning that is both fun and engaging. As your event reaches toward its climax, your audience may be searching internally through their own reactions to the content. These reactions can be complex, and the highest levels of reactions can be described as transformations. Transformations are the highest value experiences your event can strive to generate for attendees. A transformation can manifest itself as a feeling of achievement. This process may give attendees' aspirations to achieve goals in their life. Creating this unforgettable experience for in-person and virtual attendees alike will leave customers 100% satisfied with their ticket purchase.

- *Atmosphere*: Nothing beats the energy of live events and the chance interact with other event attendees, organizers and speakers. That is why people still go to sports stadiums when they can easily watch the game live on TV. There are quite a few ways you can modernize your online experience for virtual ticket viewers to provide a similar experience. You can start by creating a custom webpage theme for your embedded live video player. The online location your audience is viewing the live stream from can help set the tone and atmosphere. A custom branded app is the best for events that produce content regularly. A custom branded website is ideal for annual events that are hosted less frequently. Next you should consider ways you can provide the online audience with interactivity. For example, you can host online polls the chat room can interact with. You can display the live poll results on a projection screen in your event or digitally overlay the results on the live stream. If you set expectations correctly, you can create an engaging experience for online viewers that make them feel part of the live event.

- *Gamification*: Every event has a tribe of fans who are fanatically dedicated to the subject matter it covers. These are some of your best customers and they may even brag about attending your event with their friends and family. You can highlight your most engaged online viewers in ways that acknowledge active participation. If you host online polls or quizzes you can share the leaderboard and acknowledge online viewers who are most engaged. Gamification is a great way to engage your online audience. Crowdpurr is a great affordable online audience engagement system that our team uses regularly. Leveraging systems like Crowdpurr is a great way to bridge the gap between the virtual and in-person audiences. Audience engagement systems are great solutions for gamifying your events experience. These systems can be hosted online and incorporated into your live stream. It's not impossible to include the in-person and online attendees in a single platform experience leveraging the audience's smartphones. If you plan to use an audience polling system for example, make sure you setup your live stream with the "low latency" mode to avoid unnecessary delays between questions and answers for your online audience.

- *Professional Development*: Events serve as gathering places for the best and brightest in any field of interest. Attendance at the event helps attendees advance their careers in many ways. Many attendees place more value on the in-person event than the online version for this reason. Long distance relationships can form online with social media after the event has taken place. Consider setting up a private Facebook group for example, that can serve as a networking space for members to stay in touch in an informal yet convenient way. Facebook groups are an amazing new way to keep the digital side of your event "alive" before, during, and after your next event.

- *Networking*: In-person events are great places for networking. On the sidelines of every event, the connections that can be made generally outweigh the cost and inconvenience of attending the event in person. Audience engagement technology allows online viewers to interact beyond the simple chat room included with your live stream. Many live stream chat rooms provide decent opportunities for networking as well. Remember the days of online chat rooms? Today online chat rooms remain a significant community building tool, especially on websites such as Twitch, YouTube and Facebook. The chat room gives viewers an immediate sense of what others are saying about your event as it is happening live. For larger events, it's always a good idea to have a moderator available to temporarily ban disruptive individuals. Chatroom moderation generally needs to be done live but you can set up rules before the live stream to block lists of words. You can easily find a list of swear words that you can copy and paste into the dis-allowed list with your live streaming provider. Another great way to boost engagement is to share comments from your chat room on the live stream. Many live streaming software solutions already have integrations with Facebook that make this easy. Consider preparing your chat room moderator with a list of questions to keep the chat room engaged. A good moderator can work wonders in a chat room. It's just like having a hostess at a party. It's always a good idea to have someone pushing the chat room conversation forward on behalf of the entire event.

- *Business Opportunities*: Attending events allow businesses and individuals to expand their opportunities. This can include finding partners for strategic alliances, as well as clients, suppliers, and solution providers. If a main attraction for your event is establishing business relationships, you may want to think about your digital audience's ability to network online. Also, consider this diminished value when you price your virtual tickets. It is possible to host a video conference space for speakers to join, where the online audience can gain real-time access to speakers and attendees. At the 2020 Worship Summit, there was a live zoom video conference call for speakers to join "break-out sessions." These break-out sessions happened after each speaker's presentation. This worked out very well and it gave virtual viewers a more personal experience at the event. Usually groups over 100-200 people can get a little unmanageable. If there are more than 100-200 virtual ticket holders who want to gain access to your video conference break-out sessions, you could consider charging for this enhanced access to the event and limiting availability. This type of interactivity lets the online audience get the "facetime" they crave without having to attend in person.

Monetizing The Live Stream

So how exactly does the delivery of a pay-per-view live stream work? Event managers are used to managing webpages, ticket processing and check in. On top of the existing event manager responsibilities now you need to play for live streaming and online audience engagement.

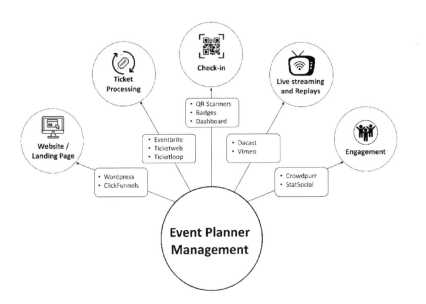

Content Delivery Network (CDN)

A CDN is a network of servers located around the world which are used to deliver content fast and securely to users. A live video streaming CDN delivers video content to all kinds of devices including smart TVs, smartphones, computers and websites. There are free and paid CDNs available to work with.

Free CDNs include streaming providers like the social media networks YouTube, Facebook, Twitter, Instagram, etc. These CDNs let you stream your content on their platforms without paying. However, since these platforms are free, you have limited controls and cannot restrict access to people who pay to watch your content. On the other hand, social media websites offer the best viewership and exposure for your event. It's always wise to use social media as part of your live streaming and virtual ticketing strategy in some way. Free live streaming platforms are generally not used for pay-per-view events. It is possible to have a private Facebook group that only paying members are let into but the process of managing this would not be automated. Using Facebook groups is a free option, but it does require a lot of user management. Most professionals will use a paid CDN for the automation and virtual ticketing solutions they offer ("Video Distribution," 2018).

Event Streaming Process

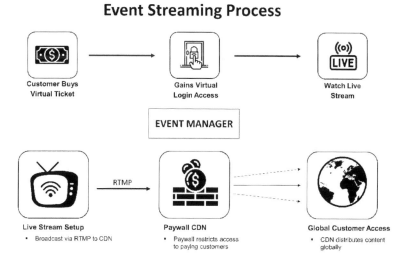

Private CDN & Paywall

Premium content delivery networks offer many important services for your live stream including a, quality of service agreements and custom branding. A private CDN allows you to restrict access to your live stream by putting the content behind a paywall. A paywall service offers you control over your intellectual property and puts tools in your hands that let you sell to anyone, almost anywhere in the world. The paywall handles all the front-end interactions with your audience regarding payment and access to your virtual event. Additionally, private CDNs offer more advanced features for custom branding which can increase engagement with your audience. Examples of private CDNs include DACAST, StreamMonkey, Vimeo and UStream ("PayWall," n.d.).

	Dacast	Ustream	StreamMonkey	Vimeo	Inplayer
Regular Price	$19/mo.	$99.00/mo.	$89/mo.	$75/mo.	$200/mo.
Storage	500GB	5TB	Unlimited	7TB	Unlimited
Monthly Bandwidth	5,000GB	4TB	Unlimited	Unlimited	Unlimited
Viewers	Unlimited	5,000/Hour	Unlimited	Unlimited	Unlimited
Quality	Full HD 1080p	HD 720p	Full HD 1080p	Full HD 1080p	Full HD 1080p
Embeddable	Yes	Yes	Yes	Yes	Yes
Customer Support	24/7	24/7	24/7	24/7	24/7
Phone Support	Yes	Yes	Yes	Yes	No
Analytics	Yes	Yes	Yes	Yes	Yes
Password Protection	Yes	Yes	Yes	Yes	Yes
Ad-free streaming	Yes	Yes	Yes	Yes	Yes
Live Chat	Yes	No	Yes	Yes	Yes

*Research done in March of 2020. Check vendor websites for up to date information.

The Event Website

The event website is an important component of the overall marketing strategy for the event. Along with providing information about the event, it serves as one of several points where potential attendees can pay for the event. Therefore, careful thought should go into how the website integrates into your overall drive to get people to sign-up and watch the live stream. What are the key aspects of the website that will facilitate this integration?

Website Payment Workflow

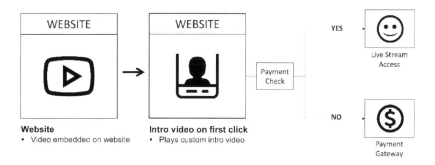

- The website should have a single source for payments. For example, if you are selling your in-person tickets via Eventbrite, it's not wise to sell the virtual tickets via the CDN's paywall. So, you should decide by testing out your options. For example, if the paywall you are using offers significant advantages to the user experience for virtual ticket holders, use them for all ticketing. Compare and contrast ticket processing as well, because most services do charge a percentage of sales for their service. If you plan on selling on-demand video access after the event, using a service like Vimeo with that feature built-in could be a significant advantage.

- Visitors to the website should not have to search for the "Buy Now" button. Ideally, it should be featured, at least twice, on every page of the website. Try placing the button on the top menu bar and then again linked throughout the site.

- Access to the live feed should not be hard to find for customers who have bought virtual tickets. New features from CDNs now allow you to embed the live stream on your homepage. They handle everything directly through the video player. You can even have a preview video explaining to the viewer that they need to pay for access with a custom intro video.

- Most premium CDNs offer complete white labeling services that you can use to customize the experience for your users. They may have a website template you can use for your entire event.

7 TICKET PRICING STRUCTURE

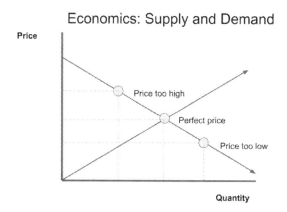

Economics: Supply and Demand

Basic economics tells us that a perfect product price does exist. The perfect price is found when supply and demand meet in a place economists call the "equilibrium." For an event, this would mean that you sell out of all your tickets and your price was high enough that you did not undercut any potential profits. Observing the law of supply and demand, in-person and virtual tickets have one fundamental difference. In-person tickets have a limited supply and virtual tickets have an unlimited supply. Each ticket type will have its own "price elasticity" which describes the product's responsiveness to changes in price. A prime example of this would be to look at a change of in-person ticket prices versus a change of the price for virtual tickets. Because in-person tickets have a limited supply, you can assume that this will drive up prices. You can also assume that the limited supply will make consumers less sensitive to price changes for this product.

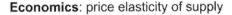

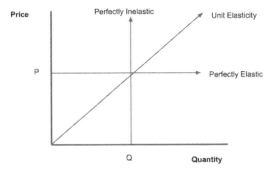

Increased profits can be achieved when ticket price and demand rise together. If the ticket prices are too high, demand for the product will go down. The goal for ticket pricing is to reach an equilibrium between price and demand. Products that are inelastic do not have customer demand that changes based on price. An example of an inelastic product would be a medicine that is needed for survival. Products that are elastic can feature large changes in consumer demand based on price. Elastic products generally not unique and have substitutes available for consumers to choose that are less expensive.

Even though virtual tickets have an unlimited supply, suppliers still must find the perfect price to reach equilibrium and therefore maximize profits. To do this consider the highest price you can charge to the largest set of potential customers. Virtual tickets have cost and therefore supply does not have to be unlimited. As you can see from the example table below, a perfect price for in-person tickets is $50. A perfect price for virtual tickets is $5. If the tickets are priced higher or lower than these equilibrium prices there is a loss in revenue.

Ticket Type	Price	Quantity	Revenue
In-Person	$100	100	$10,000
In-Person	**$50**	**500**	**$25,000**
In-Person	$10	1,000	$10,000

Virtual	$10	1,000	$10,000
Virtual	**$5**	**5,000**	**$25,000**
Virtual	$1	10,000	$10,000

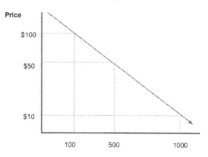

Market for in-person tickets

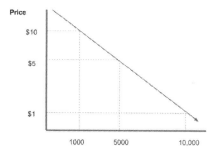

Market for virtual tickets

Tiered Levels for Tickets

Most events use a tiered ticket-pricing structure which can easily be integrated into a virtual ticket pricing strategy. Event managers often use pricing mechanisms, such as early sign-ups, referrals and group purchases to increase demand without reducing the value of a ticket. By using incentives, you can reach a wider range of customers by reducing prices temporarily.

Tier One Ticket: Free

The first ticket tier you should have for virtual access to the event is **FREE!** Although this might sound counterintuitive, it makes sense from a business point of view. By allowing users to watch a limited amount of content such as the first few minutes or hours of your event for free on social media, you will be giving interested viewers a no-risk opportunity to try out your product before they commit to paying for it. This is a great way to win over potential customers who are still hesitant about buying a virtual ticket. In addition to giving people a *try-before-you-buy* option, offering a portion of your content free allows it to be shared widely, which will greatly expand your reach and makes it possible for even more people to sign-up for the event. Furthermore, you can offer limited free access to both the virtual tickets and on-demand access to your library of content after the event. In this way, you can create a great free lead capture system with content you already have. Free tickets are a great way to capture leads before people are ready to buy. Offer free limited admission virtual tickets at the bottom of your landing page to capture folks who haven't already purchased. A free basic ticket could have limited access to a pre-show and include advertising to encourage premium ticket sales.

Ticket Pricing Options

There are three primary levels of access to an event that you can offer customers ("Private Live Streaming & Selling Virtual Tickets," n.d.).

- *In-Person Access*: This carries the highest level of urgency since it is not only time-bound, but the venue also has a limited number of people it can contain. Additionally, it offers the greatest number of benefits because in-person attendees will gain access to the content of the event, as well as direct access to other people who will be present at the venue. To maximize in-person sales, it is recommended that this tier be divided further. Suggested subdivisions are:

  - VIP access (which may offer exclusive access to conference speakers and organizers) as well as all the other benefits enjoyed by ticket holders.

  - Ticket bundles may include access to the on-demand content at lower rates and other benefits (Group Discounts).

  - General admission offers straightforward access to the event without any perks.

40

- *Virtual Tickets*: Virtual tickets also carry an element of urgency, but to a lesser degree than in-person tickets. That is because there is no limit to the number of people who can purchase virtual tickets. You can increase the value of virtual tickets by limiting supply. You can do this without affecting sales if the number is more than you expect to sell.

  - Virtual access bundled with on-demand access (offers on-demand access at a lower rate).

  - Virtual access without on-demand access.

  - Virtual access bundled with some type of VIP behind the scenes access or interview. This type of virtual ticket should always have a limited supply.

- *On-Demand Access*: This is the least urgent category of access. However, for events that take place in many rooms simultaneously, on-demand access to the event's library is almost inescapable for most attendees. This is a great option for professional teams that want to review the content later on in the year.

Other Monetization Options

- *Additional Paywall Option*: In addition to the Par-Per-View model already discussed where users pay for a one-time access to your content, there is also the subscription model. This model works best if you create new content that your audience pays for continuous access to. This can also work for on-demand access to your library of premium videos. A subscription is always better than a one-time ticket sale. You can consider offering discounts for subscriptions which essentially give the audience access to all of your events and/or premium video collection on a monthly or yearly basis ("4 Ridiculously Easy Ways to Generate Revenue with Live Video," 2018).

- *Sponsorship and Advertising*: This is another route to go, but it is only possible if you have enough viewers on your platform to make it attractive to potential advertisers. Ideally, most advertisers want platforms that have hundreds of thousands of viewers. Large numbers afford them greater exposure. Primary content sponsors may be satisfied with smaller numbers of highly qualified contacts. Most premium CDN services allow you to pay advertisements during your live stream which include analytics you can provide your sponsors.

Your Event Pricing Strategy

The way that you structure pricing for in-person and virtual tickets helps to ensure maximum profitability for your event. Therefore, each ticket type should be made attractive to a specific kind of customer and open up attendee choices to wider audiences (Team, 2019).

- People who buy virtual tickets may never attend the event in-person even if it is the only option. This is because they have real constraints which prevent them from being at the event. Modern consumers lead busy lives and for some convenience is king.

- On the other hand, attendees who prefer to be physically present at the event may not appreciate a virtual ticket, since it denies them the other benefits of being at an event in-person. You can use this to your advantage by giving in-person ticket buyers a virtual ticket to give to a friend.

- Virtual tickets can also be used as an upsell to promote physical attendance. If you price your virtual ticket very low, you will sell more. You may decide that your goal is to increase overall exposure and make the event completely free on social media. Either way, the increased exposure for your event may be used to promote in-person ticket sales long term. Viral referrals can be used to give coupons or discounts to anyone who shares the event online.

- The video footage from your live stream can be posted on social media before, during and after the event to help promote sales. Before your event starts you can create a live stream of the "pre-show" on Facebook and/or YouTube to promote virtual ticket sales with a count-down timer. During the event there are ways to easily post snippets of your event to social media. These short snippets can be set up to have a link directly to the buy page for your virtual tickets. There is a great Dropbox integration with Zapier that can be used to automatically post any videos created in a specific folder to social media. In this way, you can have a special folder that automatically posts video recordings to social media websites with custom messages and a link back to your website. After the event you can post entire segments or clips of the event to promote long term ticket sales for your next event.

- Existing customers could qualify for legacy pricing with a special coupon code. Many events suffer from the law of diminishing returns where attendees continue to get less and less out of the experiences they have already had in the past. In this case, you can continue to lower your price for repeat customers with discounts or lure them back with a fresh new virtual experience. A virtual ticket's value in convenience and price may be enough to bring back old customers who would not have otherwise purchased a ticket.

- Watch parties are a new feature used by Facebook to describe a group of friends watching a video together online. Anyone can host a watch party, invite their friends, and chat about the video in real time. Virtual ticket experiences can also be set up like this for groups of friends located around the world. Virtual ticket experiences can be set up in offices and home theaters for groups of friends. As a marketer selling virtual tickets, the idea of a watch party could powerfully explain the value of a virtual ticket to buyers. This is the type of marketing done by the NFL for the

Super Bowl. Over 100 million people tuned in to the 2020 Superbowl live broadcast. This event takes the idea of watch parties to the next level. Over 1.4 billion chicken wings were consumed, and 162 million pounds of avocados were mashed into guacamole. That's a whole lot of watch parties going on to support those record breaking numbers in 2020.

Audience Size Potential

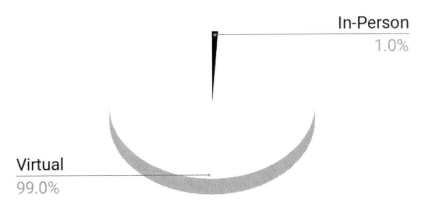

Virtual tickets will not shrink your audience. Consider your total addressable audience in the pie chart above. In most cases, less than 1% of the total addressable market can attend your event in person. It's very likely that the other 99% of the audience is willing to pay a small fee to attend your event virtually. Virtual tickets will expand the reach of your event beyond the number of people your venue can accommodate. Instead of a local audience, your event is now open to the world. At the same you are creating an additional revenue stream you can use to make the event more profitable ("Selling Event Virtual Tickets and Private Live Streams," 2017).

Categories of Virtual Access

Virtual access to an event can be real-time or post-event.

- ***Real-Time Access*** happens as the event unfolds at the venue. Real-time tickets holders join those attending the event in-person and are part of the action as it happens. This is the most exciting way to deliver access to your virtual ticket holders. This approach also requires a live video production system and a team to run it.

- *On-Demand Access* happens after the event. This is generally access to a library of event videos and premium digital assets. The experience is non-interactive but valuable, nonetheless. Attendees who paid for in-person access and real-time access often buy on-demand access as well.

- *Premiere Access* is a new style of releasing recorded videos for large audiences. YouTube, Facebook, and Twitch all feature video premiers that allow you to upload a video to be released at a certain time and date. The premiere feature includes a countdown timer and chat room for the live viewers to participate in. Premieres are a great way to release new snippets about your event in an exciting way. If you plan to upload your video anyway, why not build up some excitement with a premiere release? When your video is about to premiere, you should consider sending an email out to let people know about the premiere. A video premiere can perform very well on social media because it alerts many of your followers organically and can spread via social media quickly. By sending as many people to the premiere as possible, you can jumpstart your videos organic growth on social media. You can consider creating a custom introduction to your event with a premiere. You can have your in-person audience watch the premiere as well or use it to boost virtual ticket sales right before your event starts.

- Selling event tickets is the main source of revenue for many events. Whether or not you intend to charge a fee for your event, it's important to set a value on the tickets with some price. Expanding the ability for your event to generate income with virtual tickets, breaks out of the limits imposed by the size of the event venue and your location. There may be thousands of people who would like to attend the event but are unable to due to work, distance, or other reasons. There is no reason why they cannot participate in your event. By live streaming your event and offering virtual tickets to it, you increase your reach to a global audience. If this is your first event with virtual tickets, consider keeping the cost low. At this point your audience doesn't know what to expect and you haven't set any precedent. If you have events all the time, consider live streaming a few events for free to let the audience know what they can expect. If you only have one big day to live stream your event, make sure you know what you are doing. As you learn how to engage your online audience and successfully implement some of the strategies you will learn in this book, you can increase your value and increase your price.

- You may also choose not to charge an entrance fee if you have other ways of making money from the event, like sponsorships and advertising. For those who need to charge a gate-fee, what are the available options for maximizing your profits? ("How To Promote An Event," n.d.).

- *Make Tickets Easy to Buy*: Use event-ticketing platforms such as Eventbrite to expand your reach and have a big bright "*Register Now*" button on your website. On your social media pages and posts ensure you have a "*Get Tickets*" button and a similar "Call-To-Action" (CTA) on every post, article and email (*31 Best Ways to Sell Tickets for Your Event*, 2019)

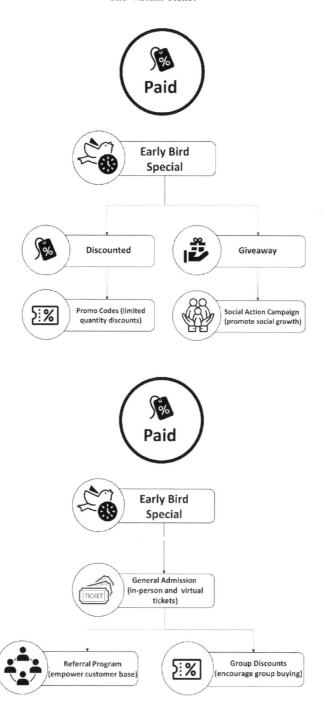

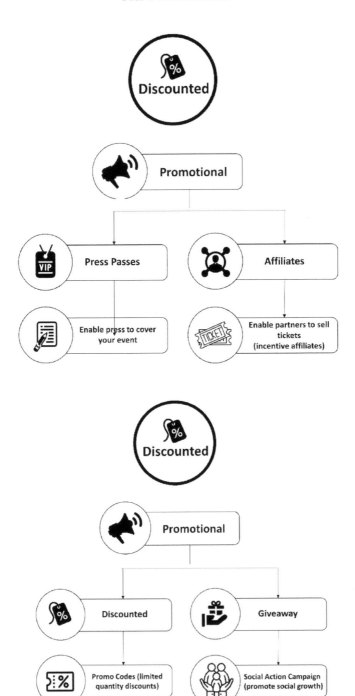

- **_Discounted Tickets_**: People who buy their tickets early should be rewarded. By making the availability of early-bird tickets limited by time, you are creating a sense of urgency. Plan out how long you will offer early bird tickets and consider extending discounts for virtual tickets well. Perhaps you will only offer behind the scenes virtual ticket passes for a limited time. Consider leveraging the new virtual ticket options to drive in-person ticket sales as well. Perhaps early-bird ticket holders also gain access to the on-demand video recordings for free. Maybe early-bird ticket holders also gain access to an exclusive night-before Q&A with the artists from their hotel room.

- **_Exclusive Offers_**: You may offer exclusive discounts to members of specific groups. People who register via your event partners' websites may be able to use a special coupon code. Live streaming and virtual tickets are still new concepts. Consider using coupon codes like "virtualticket" or "livestream" to reinforce the virtual ticket concept on social media.

- **_Special Tickets_**: Discounted group tickets also let people band together to buy tickets at a lower price. If you have a professional conference, you can promote the idea of setting up an entire office "Lunch and Learn" to view the live stream. Now that people are watching your event from home, there are plenty of ways you can get viewers excited about their exclusive access capabilities. Just because you are selling virtual tickets, doesn't mean that you can't send your customers real tickets in the mail. Having a physical ticket is a great prop that you can use for social media campaigns. For the 2020 Worship Summit, we mailed out over 1,000 free virtual tickets to churches around the country. You can use email or direct mail to make the experience of receiving a virtual ticket more exciting for customers.

- **_Ticket Bundles_**: Offer something in addition to the event tickets. Consider the value of a virtual ticket and allow attendees to give one friend a free pass if it makes sense. If your main goal is to sell in person tickets, the virtual ticket might be a way to get more referrals from your existing customers. Consider bundling in-person tickets, with virtual tickets and/or on-demand video access to the recordings. Even if you must charge for each type individually, consider offering discounted bundles and referral options that will increase profits overall. If you are mailing out customer tickets, include two free virtual tickets to promote referrals.

- **_Ticket Giveaways_**: Free tickets allow you to setup giveaways that can steer additional attention to your event. For the 2019 StreamGeeks Summit, we used a service called Gleam.io to host a giveaway where entries required people to make social media actions. In our case, in order to enter the giveaway users had to share the event on social media, comment on a video and retweet a specific twitter post. The buzz you will generate will more than make up for whatever you are giving away.

- **_Use referrals_**: Offer discounts to potential attendees who can get others to sign up for the event. You can set up affiliate programs for organizations who may be able to send you a large number of interested buyers. Also consider ways to give your ticket buyers the opportunity to gain something for referring a friend. Acquiring a customer via a referral has many benefits over other acquisition methods. Studies show that referral customers have a longer lifetime value, they are more loyal, and they are less expensive to acquire. All of this adds up to a significantly higher ROI for acquiring referral business over new customers.

- **_Lead Capture_**: With virtual ticketing you have a lot of options to capture leads and upsell access to the main event. For example, you can live stream a pre-show or a behind the scenes talk with one of your keynote speakers. For non-exclusive content, it's okay to live stream it directly to social media websites like Facebook and YouTube. During promotional streams, you can ask for viewers to share the live stream and enter for a chance to win a free ticket. Live streaming to social media websites is 100% free, and it offers you maximum reach into online audiences. Derral Eves used this strategy to drive traffic to his virtual ticket buy page, even when his event was totally sold. Now that is an entrepreneur. Check to see if one of your keynote speakers or main event entertainers would like to leverage their social media channels to make some extra money. Using a service such as ClickFunnels you can quickly set up an affiliate landing page that can pay out a set percentage of the sales to your partners.

- **_Promotional:_** Many of these behind the scenes live streams work well with an IRL setup. IRL stands for "In Real Life" and in the live streaming world this means a mobile backpack streaming setup. You can learn about the StreamGeeks IRL backpack setup at streamgeeks.us/IRL. These mobile backpacks are ideal for live streaming from any place, at any time, using a cellular connection. The mobile backpack is usually set up in advance to stream directly to any social media website or private server that you set up. In our case, we generally set up our IRL backpack to live stream to a service called GoEasyLive which allows us to overlay graphics and restream to multiple websites. If you have the goal of upselling viewers to purchase virtual tickets, it's a good idea to have a lower thirds banner to direct viewers to the URL you want them to purchase from.

Live Stream Promotion Strategy

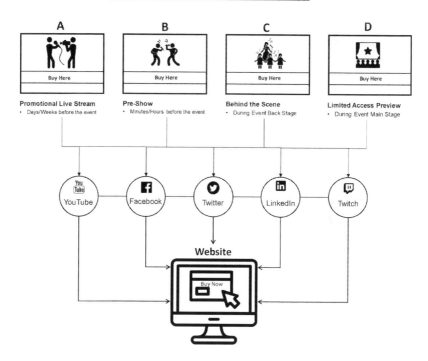

8 PREPARING YOUR EVENT FOR THE LIVE STREAM

*If I were given one hour to save the planet, I would spend 59 minutes defining the problem and one minute resolving it," ...*Albert Einstein

Attending an event is always more exciting than the process of planning it. Nobody minds going to a party, but who wants to deal with all the little details about cleaning the venue, making sure there is good parking or proofreading invitations before they are sent out. However, even though the activities that take place before an event are not exciting, they lay the groundwork for how enjoyable the actual event will be. As an event planner, if you want to enjoy the event, you must pay attention to planning it. And no aspect of planning is more important than the pre-planning. This is when you decide why you want to have the event, who the audience will be, and if you can pull it off with the resources you have available to you.

Event Feasibility

Event Goals & Objectives: Why Is The Event Important?

There is nothing worse than an ill-conceived event. It is not uncommon for individuals and businesses to decide on a spur of the moment to have an event. When you are planning an event it's all about asking the right questions and defining your expectations. It's important to understand during the pre-planning stages that the event objective will likely change over time. You may even decide to abandon the project for various reasons along the way. Think critically about your event because the first time will likely be the hardest. Future events will be much easier to host once you have established the event framework. Some things will only become clear to you during the planning process. Others may not become clear until after your event is over. The goal of pre-planning is to uncover as much information as possible to steer your event toward a successful future.

Determine the business problem your event will solve. This is the most important step of any event because it will help to secure the event's success for yourself and the attendees. The business problem or the need which an event aims to satisfy helps to confine your efforts during the planning stage to only what is valuable for fulfilling that outcome. Think about your online audience during this process. Will you be able to give online viewers access to an experience that fulfills their expected outcomes?

You can assume online viewers understand they will not have access to in-person experiences such as networking. But can you compensate them in some ways by providing behind the scenes access to the keynote speaker? Perhaps your virtual ticket holders can ask questions during the presentation's Q&A session. Are there ways that you can give your virtual ticket holders a private online group for networking with attendees online? After all, LinkedIn has over 660 million members. Perhaps you can create a LinkedIn networking group to help encourage collaboration for members of your event. To determine if the event will become a successful business, ask the following questions (unless the event is something personal, like a wedding, retirement party or a hangout for family and friends):

- Who needs what the event offers?

- Are there enough of these people to justify holding the event?

- How many in-person attendees do you estimate versus virtual attendees?

- Do you have the means to reach these people?

- Will the outcome justify the effort and cost of creating the event?

- Do you have the capacity to hold such an event?

- Should you have the event?

The more painstaking and exact the answers to these questions are, the greater clarity the project will have, and the more guided future decisions and actions will be (Spradlin, 2012). During the research for writing this book, I was fixated on hosting an event in New York City where the virtual ticket experience would come as close as possible to the in-person experience. While the event was a massive successful for all parties involved, I realized only after the event that an all online approach could cost one fifth the price and potentially reach more people. Four months later, the StreamGeeks hosted the 2020 Worship Summit which sold more virtual tickets than the StreamGeeks Summit in less time with a much lower budget. It was interesting to see the highest ROI came from catering directly to an online audience.

Write down your answers to the questions about the event. The next step is to crystalize your ideas by making them more specific in terms of time, budget and other resources. What are the things you need to successfully hold this event and are they readily available? If they are not available, can they be obtained?

Event Budget

In establishing a budget, remember that everything has a cost, even if you will use volunteers. The list of your costs should be comprehensive. It's better to overestimate than underestimate. However, if costs get too high, the event may stop being feasible. Adding live streaming equipment, operators, and virtual ticket processing to your costs early on is a good idea. You will have to come up with a balance between your expected virtual ticket sales and the cost of adding live streaming to your event. Some events now add live streaming as a free promotional tool and absorb the costs for live streaming the event. Proper costing involves a detailed breakdown of all that is needed for the event, attaching a monetary value, and then making room for contingencies. Having access to someone experienced at creating such events will ensure you are moving in the right direction. Later, in this book you will review various DIY video production systems and ballpark pricing estimates from production companies (Colston, 2018). If you are unsure about the budget for live streaming, reach out to the venues' recommended rental/staging and AV company vendor. Below are the costs for the audio visuals from the 2019 StreamGeeks Summit.

Location	Description	Price
Audio	Behringer X32 Producer Digital Console. Wireless Podium Mic. 6 Shure Digital Wireless Microphones. Computer Audio Package. In-House Sound System Connection. All necessary cabling and adapters.	$3,140.00
Video	Analog Way Quick Vu HD Switcher. Seamless Presentation Switcher. In-House Display Connection. All necessary cabling and adapters.	$2,000.00

Lighting	Gallery Stage Lighting Package. Front Stage Wash Lighting System from Ceiling.	Included
Staging	4'x8' Stage Deck (Grey Carpet) 8x20 Stage - 12" High Black Skirting.	Included
Power	100amp 3 Phase Power Distro	Included
Labor	Lighting Technician. AV Specialists. AV Technician.	$4,385.00
Live Streaming	Producer/Technical Director. Video Switcher. HD recorders.	$5,425.00
Total		$14,950.00

*New York City is one of the most expensive cities in the world to hire outside contractors. Prices in other cities around the world will likely be less expensive.

Sponsors & Partners

Depending on the type of event, it is possible to find organizations that are willing to put their name and money behind your event. This is very commonly a win-win for events and brands who are in similar industries. However, to attract sponsorship, the business problem your event addresses, and the kind of people it will attract, must line up with the interests of any potential sponsors. Furthermore, the event must give the organization enough exposure to warrant their involvement. Taking into consideration what a company needs will make your event sponsorship proposal more compelling. Sponsors would generally like to hear that the event will be live streamed online. You can decide to live stream any portion of your event directly to a sponsor's social media pages such as Facebook or YouTube to add extra value. Many top-tier events are now live streaming their conferences for free to add this type of additional exposure for their sponsors. At the 2020 Worship Summit, the entire conference stream was free, and the way in which attendees obtained virtual tickets acted as the lead capture method for sponsors ("How to Secure Event Sponsorship," 2019).

Set A Date

Do not choose your event date randomly. If you set the date when your target audience is unavailable (e.g., during vacation season when targeting families), your event will likely flop. Avoid dates where major events that target the same audience will be held. Also, check for the availability of key speakers or guests whom you need to be at the event. Your target date may also be subject to the venue's availability. Do not rush your event to fit someone else's schedule. Give yourself enough time for planning, making mistakes and recovering from them.

Licenses, Permits, etc

What could be worse than working hard to plan an event, only to get busted at the venue on account of your failure to get the necessary government permits? Permits are a necessary part of many events and there is hardly any public event which does not require them. Make a list of the permits you are likely to need in the pre-planning stages. If you are live streaming your event, you will have to consider licensing in new ways. Your live stream could be shut down or flagged due to a copyright violation for music that is playing in-between speakers. There are many royalty-free options for music that you will want to review before having your live stream shut-down inadvertently (Hunt, 2015).

Important Venue considerations

A venue can make or break an event. All your efforts to find sponsors and choose the right dates for the event will mean nothing if your venue is unavailable for your chosen date. Locking down a good venue is one of the most important pieces of your event-planning equation. It allows you to plan out the other elements of the process with some certainty. What are the factors to take into consideration in deciding if a venue is right? ("Evaluating an Event Venue," 2018).

- **Venue:** Draw up a list of potential venues based on these three factors and then use the other factors in this list to choose the best venue.

- **Cost:** Factors that may affect the cost of venue include time of the year and day of the week.

- **Transport and Parking**: How easy is it to get to the venue? Is there enough parking?

- **Required equipment**: Do you have enough space and support for the equipment you will need? Where can you place the audio/video desk? Where will you place the live streaming cameras and microphones?

- **Internet Connection**: Even if you do not intend to use it, it is good to know that the internet is available. Generally, you will want a hard-wired ethernet connection for live streaming with a minimum of 5-10Mbps of upload/download speeds.

- **Audience Arrangement:** The layout of the venue is important. Are there layout options that are more conducive to capturing your live streamed experience?

- **Other Considerations**: Health and Safety (Security, Insurance, Sanitation, etc).

- **Audio Visuals**: Does the venue have installed audio visual equipment you can gain access to? Is there a preferred audio-visual vendor you can work with?

Event Branding

To create an association between your event and the experience, product or service it represents, you should brand your event accordingly. No doubt there are similar events that are also being promoted to the same audience you are catering to. How do you make your event stand out in the minds of people? Start by making a unique promise and presenting your event as offering something extra special. The goal of branding is that your name comes to mind when people think of a experience. Your branding should remain consistent throughout all elements of your event including your website, social media, video production, signage, printed materials and messaging ("The Ultimate Guide to Event Branding | Eventbrite," 2019). There are many components to branding an event; the key ones are listed below ("20 Event Branding Tips To Run Your Next Event," 2016).

- Event Name: Evocative and easy to recall.

- Unique Logo: Distinct and recognizable.

- <u>The Tagline</u>: Memorable and communicating what the event is about.

- <u>Font/Theme/Colors</u>: In sync with your message and the mood you want to create.

- <u>Consistency</u>: The same message and images across all touchpoints.

- <u>Website</u>: Everything above should be integrated into a clean and consistent website.

- <u>Video Production</u>: The images and assets created for your event should make their way into the live stream and video production branding as well.

- <u>Social Media</u>: Your social media strategy should incorporate all your branding initiatives and portray your core messaging properly.

- <u>Throwable Microphones</u>: You can now purchase throwable microphones that are perfect for Q&A sessions. These microphones can be branded with your events logo.

9 BUILDING A TEAM

Success as an event planner depends on a person's level of precision. The more exact event planners are about all aspects of the project, the better they will be at planning it. Having determined the foundational framework for your event, you can now create a team.

Assembling Your Team And Finding Your Key Personnel

All events need the right kind of people to succeed. This includes external partners, as well as the event-planning team members. To attract external partners, your internal team must be professional enough to inspire outsiders' confidence. Bringing the right people into the planning process is vital to the event's success. Below are indispensable qualities to look out for in team members.

- Commitment and Reliability: Team members should have a stake in the success of the event. Event-planning is rife with uncertainty, so you want lots of stability in your team.

- Expertise vs. Availability: Sometimes you have to make a tradeoff between ability and availability. An expert who is unavailable is of no use to you.

- Able To Handle Pressure: Event-planners must think on their feet, be resourceful and respond with speed.

- Teamwork: An event planning team is all about synergy and teamwork. Try to build a team of people who complement each other.

To create an effective team, pinpoint the skills that are indispensable to your event and give them priority. If you are planning to sell lots of virtual tickets, make sure to prioritize your team's access to video production professionals. Audio visual teams will have their own set of requirements for success. If you are planning to sell lots of on-demand video recordings make sure you are accounting for the audio-visual gear and knowhow necessary to capture the event via video. The must-have skills required for your event may vary, but most events will need the following roles (Kaiser, 2018).

The Event Director: Oversees everything and is usually responsible for communicating with external partners.

Creative Team: Various team members who are responsible for branding the event and producing its communication materials. This team manages website development, social media, and content creation.

Treasury: Oversees budget implementation and disbursement of funds.

Operations and Logistics: In charge of transportation, supplies, venue management, crowd management, parking, security, etc.

Technical Team: Manages technology aspects of the event; equipment setup, video, displays, sound, lighting, and power. Someone on this team should be in close contact with your creative team in order to properly brand your live video streams and recordings.

Catering: Responsible for creating the menu, plus food preparation, delivery and service.

Marketing and Sales: In charge of promotions; social media, ads placements, dispatch of invitations, email, ticketing, etc. This may include PR (Public Relations) and the drafting of press releases. It's important to make your event available to any members of the press that may be interested in attending.

Entertainment: The role explains itself. This may include a host for your online audience and live stream. This role could also include a host who keeps the flow of event moving in-between sessions.

10 CREATING THE EVENT SCOPE OF WORK

Because events have many moving parts, overlooking something vital is a constant danger. Attempting to keep all tasks that go into planning the event in your head is inefficient. You don't want important tasks to get buried under a pile of less important things that feel more urgent. There is an objective tool for keeping tabs on all the parts of your event without getting overwhelmed; the WORK BREAKDOWN STRUCTURE or WBS.

A WBS takes everything your project is supposed to create, sorts them into a hierarchical arrangement, and then displays them graphically. Each element of work that needs to be done is identified and positioned below the work before it and above the work after it. This type of job scope helps streamline team communication effectively. To create a work breakdown structure, here are the steps to follow. (Cohen, n.d.). ("What is a Work Breakdown Structure (WBS)—Workbreakdownstructure.com," n.d.).

Decomposition:

- Step 1: Write your event at the top of a blank sheet of paper or whiteboard (as if you were about to draw an organizational chart). The event forms the first level of the chart.

- Step 2: Now list the major things which must be accomplished to make the event successful; the live stream, event branding, sponsorship, etc. These make up the second level of the WBS.

- Step 3: Under each outcome or product, list all the elementary tasks necessary to create that outcome or product. For example, each individual task needs to be successfully branded for the event.

The WBS is highly detailed by design. Its effectiveness is dependent on how much work goes into outlining the tasks under each level, which brings us to the WBS rules ("Work Breakdown Structure (WBS) Examples," 2007).

The 100% Rule: It states that your Work Breakdown Structure must contain 100% of the tasks that are included within the project. In other words, no task can be excluded.

Deliverable: This defines a specific product, outcome or service that must be created before any task listed on the WBS can be considered as finished.

Below are the two important characteristics of the WBS (Cohen, n.d.). It's nice to start this process with your entire team. Consider using a large white board space where everyone can collaborate. Eventually you will want this information available in a shared document that can easily be updated and referenced by your entire team.

- <u>Hierarchy</u>: Elements of the WBS must be arranged sequentially below their appropriate levels.

- <u>Mutually Exclusive</u>: Elements must be mutually exclusive to avoid duplication.

Managing The Event-Planning Team

After you have assembled your team, a team structure is essential to ensure efficiency. One of the easiest ways to introduce conflict into a team workflow is to fail to provide clarity about each person's roles and responsibilities. Although every event planning team will be different there are the basic elements to structuring the team.

Job Descriptions: Every team member needs a job description (JD). A job description offers clarity and direction for each member of your team and their co-workers. It must be unambiguous and exclusive ("Event Management: Structure of an event management team," n.d.).

Organization Chart: The chart should show team hierarchy and the flow of authority within the group, so that individuals know who they report to. Include important outside contractors in this list and connect them with the team member responsible for managing their work.

Communication: Effective communication is the glue that keeps the group in sync. A clear event job scope paired with an online collaboration system is a great way to keep track of team progress.

Establish Your KPIs: Key Performance Indicators offer an objective way to measure your team's progress and decide on the next course of action ("What is a KPI?," n.d.).

Monitor: The RACI (Responsible, Accountable, Consulted and Informed) model can help you determine exactly who is involved with a task and what their level of responsibility is ("Role Up, Roll Out," n.d.). Monitoring an online collaboration software like Slack or Discord has become a very popular way for teams small and large to stay informed.

Creating An Event-Planning Schedule

Creating an event planning schedule is a great starting point for organizing packing lists and drilling down into the finer details of event implementation. Without a schedule, team members can gravitate to tasks that make sense but lack order. With a system that keeps track of time relationships between tasks, it is possible to impose order and have team members help out where things may be falling behind. This allows your approach to be logical and sequential, and your whole team can move in unison toward the event goals.

The Gantt Chart

A Gantt Chart is another project management tool that can make the lives of event planners easier. The Gantt Chart helps to create a clear timeline of the important pieces of the planning process. The chart makes it super-easy to follow the team's progress and ensures important deadlines are met. It shows the relationship, in terms of time, between the different elements of your event plan. Gantt Charts are easy to create and because they are intuitive, people do not need to be experts to understand them. Even better, you can create one using tools or materials you already have. Depending on the complexity of your event, you can use a whiteboard or a software like Google Slides to make your Gantt Chart. ("Event Gantt Chart Overview and Example," 2007).

The Packing List

At the 2019 StreamGeeks Summit, the setup team used a detailed packing list to reference during planning and setup. A packing list is used to organize everything the team needs to put the event together. The packing list is essential for organization and transporting all of your gear to the event site without forgetting anything. This is especially important if you plan to put together the live streaming system yourself. It is also helpful to label boxes and other equipment with a label maker that notes the area where each item should be delivered.

Before you arrive to set everything up, you should always plan a few meetings to review the packing list. Communication is key when you have multiple people on your team working together. In your meetings, you should be reviewing the layout, the equipment list, and the execution plan. If you have multiple areas of your event it can be helpful to make separate packing lists for each area.

Here is an example of the packing list for the 2019 StreamGeeks Summit:

Esports Section	TriCaster Section	Wirecast Stream	Esports Production Section	Registration Booth Section	WorkShop Section

(X4) PowerStrips	(X2) PowerStrip	(X1) 24-Port Switch #1	(X1) PowerStrip	(X250) Lanyards	(X1) vmix System
(2 each station)	(X3) NDI PTZ Optics	(X1) NETWORK SETUP	(X1) Step and Repeat	(X250) Name Tags	(X1) PowerStrip
(X2) Banners	(X3) Speaker Stands	(X1) WIFI SETUP	(X1) Observer PC	(X2) Pens	(X1) Keyboard Mouse
(X4) Banner Tripods	(X1) 24-Port Switch #2	(X1) 12X NDI Zcam	(X1) Keyboard & mouse	(X2) Markers	(X1) 20X-SDI Camera
(X6) PTZ WebCams	(X1) Tricaster System	(X1) Wirecast Gear	(X2) MICROPHONES	(X1) Guest List	(X1) PoE Switch
(X6) Computers	(X1) Confidence Mon.	(X1) Audio Mixer	(X2) MIC STANDS		(X1) Audio System
(X6) Keyboards	(X1) SDI to HDMI Conv.	(X1) KEYBOARD MOUSE	(X2) XLR CABLES		
(X6) Mices	(X1) Monitor Stand	(X1) NDI ARCADE	(X1) BROADCAST DESK		
(X6) HeadSets	(X1) KEYBOARD MOUSE	(X1) LCD MONITOR			
(X6) Ethernet Cables	(X1) MAGEWELL NDI CAPTURE	(x1) OBS Streaming PC			

A packing list like this can be used to assist in organizing your "day of" preparations. Once your packing list is made up, review it with your team so that you are not the only person who knows where everything is supposed to go. Once you have your packing list in place, it's time to create your day-of to-do list. This is a list of everything that needs to be done, at what time, and by whom. Take a look at the following list from the 2019 StreamGeeks Summit.

Event Execution Schedule

Time	Activity	Person	Details
4:30	Delivery of equipment from hotel rooms to Gallery	Paul/Melissa	Request Carts from Hotel night before
4:30	Uber Eats Coffee Massive Delivery Order	Michael	
5:00 AM	Stage Build / AV & Lighting	AV Workshop	AV Workshop our vendor to handle
5:00 AM	Running Power (Center Streaming Areas + Esports)	Paul/Melissa/Andy	Run Power Cables and Power Strips to each major streaming area
5:30 AM	Cable Runs & Gaff Tape Down	Melissa, Stuart	Melissa to set up streaming system with help from team
5:30 AM	Workshop Setup	Andy	vMix System, PTZOptics Camera on Tripod, Microphone on Stand, Projector connected
5:30 AM	ESports System Setup	Todd Conley / Helix Esports	Plug in all computer and booth them up. Connect them to network cables
5:30 AM	Speaker Stand Setup / Banner Setup	Sean, Kyle	Speaker Stands are for cameras. Use 1/4-20 screws. Banners are above Esports areas and use 3 tripods and center pole
5:30 AM	Broadcast Table Pop Up / 10' Step and Repeat Banner	Matt / Pat	Instructions in bags. This goes next to Esports table. Setup table and LCD on it with Observer PC.
5:30 AM	Press Area Set up	Julia	Posters and Easels. Sponsors (on Columns). Schedules / Media Space
6:00 AM	Table / Chair Arrangements	All Teams	All teams may need to help arrange tables with tech on them. They need to be in place to go further in our setup plans
6:00 AM	Confidence Monitor setup SDI to HDMI	Matt/Pat	Build cart and connect SDI to HDMI converter. Connect

			power strip to converter and LCD. Put camera on top
6:00 AM	LED Screen Setup	Be Terrific	One LCD in lobby and one next to Esports areas
6:00 AM	Network Configuration	Matt Davis	Should be plug and play. Review IP connections for all computers.
6:00 AM	Poster & Easel Set Up	Tess	Posters and Easels. Sponsors (on Columns). Schedules / Media Space
6:00 AM	MP3 Files on USB Stick (Test Laptop) Play Music on House Speakers	Tess	Play music to get team moving this early in the morning
6:30 AM	Wirecast Streaming System Setup (Camera Focus)	Melissa / Paul Richards	Make sure Wirecast machine is connected to all cameras and working.
6:30 AM	OBS Streaming System Testing (Esports Focus)	Todd Conley	
6:30 AM	Audio System Testing (Esports Area)	Melissa	
6:30 AM	TriCaster Steaming System Testing	John Mahoney	
7:00 AM	LiveU Stream Setup #1	Paul	Setup LiveU with Wirecast and make sure it's streaming properly
7:15 AM	LiveU Stream Setup #2	Paul	Setup LiveU with TriCaster and make sure it's streaming properly
7:00 AM	Registration Area Setup	Sean, Kyle	Set out badges and lanyards
7:00 AM	Streaminng System Testing	Paul / Matt / Andy	Check to see if all NDI sources needed are available properly
7:00 AM	PTZOptics Booth Setup (PTZO Backdrop)	Matt / Pat	Partner Team to layout display and brochures
7:00 AM	Book Signing Area	Tess	Books should be out and ready with a small sign

Time	Task	Person	Notes
7:00 AM	Placement of signage (Small Signs for each area)	Julia	Final check over everything.
7:30 AM	Empty Box removal	Julia / Tess	Can we move empty boxes and cartons to the Workshop area or press room?
8:00 AM	General Testing	Everybody	
8:00 AM	Microphone Test	Tess	
8:00 AM	Powerpoint / Projector Test	Sean	
8:00 AM	Start Streaming and Test EasyLive	Tess / Paul	Use Wirecast Computer to log into EasyLive... Check streams and start them
8:30 AM	Paul & Tess Get on stage - Test Microphones	Paul / Tess	**Review announcement speech**
8:45 AM	Paul makes a short speech	Paul	Play short video and presentation #1
9:00 AM	Facebook Panel Starts	Tess	Take speakers onto stage
9:45 AM	Catchbox used for Q&A	Tess	Throw catch box into the crowd
10:00 AM	Business Panel	Paul	Usher next panel onto the stage
11:00 AM	Esports Tournament	Tess	Prepare for Esports Play-by-Play Announcements

Staying organized is the key to successful events. Above, you can see each task starts with the time that the task should be executed. It's important to have someone on your team who is responsible for keeping everyone on pace with the schedule. This person is usually found with a clipboard, checking off completed tasks and helping along team members who have questions about next steps.

11 EVENT MARKETING AND PUBLICITY

The marketing for your event should be approached strategically and systematically. Anything short of a good strategy can easily result in lots of work with no real progress. Sure, you may be able to drive traffic to your event's landing page, but is your call to action compelling enough to convert those visitors into paying customers? An intelligently designed event marketing/publicity program should be able to boil down your event's value into a short memorable elevator pitch. The elevator pitch is a message that addresses the main problem your event will solve in 30 seconds or less. A compelling elevator pitch is essential for helping your entire team, partners, and affiliates explain to others via word of mouth and social media, what your event is all about.

If you are just starting out, look for events like yours and see how they are positioning their events. What are the buzzwords that they are using? How are they describing the event? Many times, it's just as important to explain what your event will not be, as it is to explain what it will be. For the 2019 StreamGeeks Summit, the website starts out explaining that this event will "not be just another consumer electronics show." Delivering your value proposition with a clean and responsive website is incredibly important. Almost all tickets, in-person and virtual, will be sold online. Your website will be where 99% of your attendees learn about your event. Consider including a countdown timer on the webpage as soon as you have determined the exact date for your event. You will want to convey a sense of urgency and exclusivity for your event, even if you do have an unlimited number of virtual tickets that you are selling. Consider planning to sell early bird tickets with limited time discounts to help drive sales early on in your marketing process. As you get closer to the date of your event you can start to market the exclusivity and limited amount of tickets available for your event to increase sales ("How to Create an Event Marketing Plan," 2019).

The Event Promotional Plan

The promotion plan is essential for your event. It makes the hard work of planning worth it. The primary goal of creating any event is to have people attend or watch online. Without people, regardless of what else you achieve, there is no event. Since marketing helps you solve the problem of reaching people and convincing them to attend the event, it is a central pillar of the event planning process. How do you garner enough attention surrounding the event to get people to buy tickets?

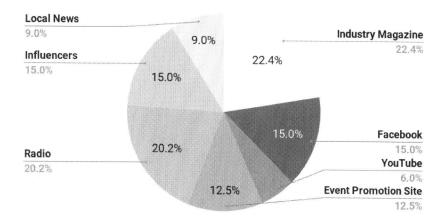

The pie chart above shows the budget allocation for the 2019 StreamGeeks Summit. As you can see the most expensive items are marketing solutions with established distribution channels to highly targeted audiences. Industry magazines and radio stations offered our marketing team audiences that were targeted for the NYC area. It's always difficult to measure exactly which advertising source generated the most business. But, after spending over $15,000 on marketing the event, I do believe that influencers and social media gave us the best return on investment.

Social media is an obvious first place to consider marketing an event. But before you go spending your social media budget, make sure your creative works. The "creative" is an industry term for the catchy phrase, image or video that you have created to get people's attention. Good creative ideas are worth sharing, dull marketing is just boring. The difference between marketing with a good creative idea versus a mediocre one is incredible. It's the difference between sailing with the wind behind your back or facing head-winds at every turn. You only need one amazing creative idea to break through the clutter of social media and email. With this in mind it's worth taking the time to do something out of the box. Whatever your idea becomes it should be used to gain the competitive edge your campaign needs to succeed. Think about how your event will stand out from the crowd. Is there a celebrity that would absolutely embody your message? Maybe you can't afford to have a celebrity host the keynote speech, but they may be willing to tell a funny joke about your event on video for $250 and share it on social media. It could be one eye-catching image, or a short video. Whatever it is, don't go spending your marketing budget without a creative idea that you believe in.

Also, consider running multiple test campaigns before you shoot for the moon. On Facebook, you can test out multiple creative ideas and see what people respond to on a very small budget. Consider changing your creative and your ad audience with multiple small budget test series. You can run A/B tests for the copy (the text written in your advertisement post), the images you use, the videos you use, and the audiences you choose. Once you have tested various advertisements you can start to expand your budget. You may want to have different ad campaigns running to promote in-person tickets versus virtual tickets. You may want to remarket a virtual ticket campaign against engaged audiences who have not yet purchased a ticket to your event. This audience may be more likely to purchase a virtual ticket because they are still on the fence about attending in person.

Calculate your ROI for a ticket sold. Then determine the cost of a lead generated through your marketing campaign. Facebook and Google both offer online tracking tools you can use to follow a lead from an ad to a sale. These tools offer the ability to give leads a value via conversion tracking. Someone on your team should be assigning conversion tracking values in both Facebook and Google Ads. Try running multiple campaigns for low daily budgets until you can see a clear winner. Once you have determined the best advertising method to convert the most sales, focus your budget on what is working ("How to Market an Event," 2015).

The Number One Factor: Know Your Event

Knowing your event is more than simply about knowing what you want to do. It is about the people for whom you want to attend the event and why they should spend their precious time attending. Your target audience determines the tone of voice you adopt in your marketing, along with your choice of marketing channels. By drilling down to the most basic details of your audience, you will get an idea of the kind of communication that will appeal to your audience. If you are getting good engagement with your advertisements, read the comments. End user feedback can lead to valuable insights you can use to tweak your approach or uncover misconceptions about your messaging. Always have someone on your team reply to comments on your social media posts. Your team can increase engagement by asking simple questions to learn more from people who are taking notice of your event online. Consider reaching out and contacting your customer list. See if some of your customers can spare some time to explain their buying decisions. Listen to your customers and ask thoughtful questions about their buying habits. You may be surprised what you learn hearing directly from customers who have purchased tickets to your event.

Your Event Brand

Your brand is not just an identity; it is a primary marketing tool. It offers avenues for articulating your event's value proposition. Your brand lets you speak in terms that resonate with your audience, and it positions you as an organization that cares about the same things as your attendees. By branding your event correctly, a good deal of the work of winning over your audience is already done. Since the brand has created the right impression in their minds, all other things - such as, timing, travel distance, urgency, costs, convenience, etc - become details to be resolved later. Once your attendees decide they want to align with your brand, their ticket choices become more important. This is where event goers start to decide whether they can come in person, purchase a virtual ticket, or at least commit to on-demand video replays.

The Event Website

Your event needs its own website, even if your organization already has a website and especially if it is an annual event. Establishing a new website takes time. Starting a blog for the website is no small feat. If you can leverage a pre-existing website to drive traffic to your event website or landing page that is always a good idea. If you are concerned about having too many websites, you can create a unique URL for the event and redirect it to the event page on your existing website. You can also use a landing page service such as ClickFunnels which can optimize your page for online sales. The website you build should at the very minimum contain a proper description of the event along with shareable pictures and images from past events, short bios of speakers, partners' logos and and a prominent "Register Now" button (even if entry is free). The better job you do explaining your event on your website, the fewer questions you will have to answer via email, chat, and phone. If there is a suggested hotel or group discount for attendees to use let people know online. This is the first-place people will look for information about your event.

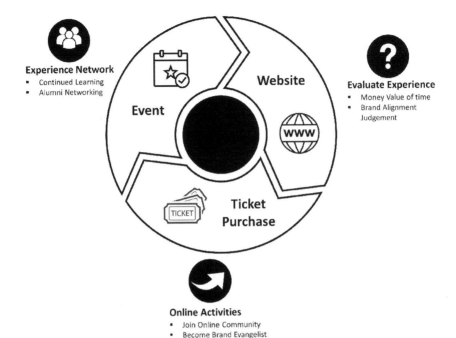

Experience Network
- Continued Learning
- Alumni Networking

Website

Event

Evaluate Experience
- Money Value of time
- Brand Alignment Judgement

Ticket Purchase

Online Activities
- Join Online Community
- Become Brand Evangelist

Essential Elements of The Plan

Choosing Your Channels: Your target audience determines the most effective marketing channels. By understanding their behavior and habits, you can zero in on the best channels to focus on. When choosing the mix of channels to use, the goal should be to create an immersive experience for your audience. You will need to create sufficient exposure to the event message until it registers in their subconscious. This means your message has to grab not only attention; it must be evocative and be replicated in different ways across different channels. Many studies show that it can take a minimum of 6-8 different marketing touches for a consumer to make a buying decision.

Email Marketing: Regardless of your overall strategy, you cannot ignore email marketing. Email is relatively cheap and if done right, it can deliver your call to action directly to your target's inbox. Email is by far the most effective marketing strategy for selling tickets, but you may not have the ideal email list to send your message to. You can consider working with a marketing company that "rents" their email list for an email "blast" to their targeted email list. Consider checking out online publications that are in your industry. Many magazines offer marketing packages you can use that include access to their email list. You should also be building your own email list. You can give away free downloadable materials or chances to win free tickets to the event in exchange for email addresses. Always have a form on your website collecting emails. Today, you need to have a compelling reason for website visitors to submit their contact information. Consider creating a piece of "hero content" like a free PDF book downloadable or a contest entry. Brainstorm about offers you can make to your audience in order to grow your email list. As your email list grows, see if you can segment your lists. The better you separate your lists, the more tailored your email marketing messages can become.

Have an Event Content Strategy: This is important during the buildup of your event and serves to inform and educate potential attendees. Content like blog posts, videos, interviews and infomercials move the engagement from promotional to conversational. You want to make people aware of the event as naturally as possible. The best-case scenario for this would be a friend hearing about your event from another friend. In the world of social media, this happens by friends sharing content with other friends. Consider hosting a few live streams where you interview key people involved with your event. Host a Q&A or create a short video that you can post during your marketing campaign to keep the conversation about your event moving forward.

Use Influencer Marketing: An influencer is viewed as an expert in a specific subject matter. With social media today, influencers are magnets for people who are interested in niche topics and they can attract attention in large numbers. By partnering with influencers, you can gain access to their followers, and win trust through an association with someone people respect. Using the 2020 Worship Summit as an example, the budget included $20,000 for advertising with a paid magazine called "Church Production." We also had $3,000 set aside for influencer marketing. After seeing the results, it was clear that the influencer marketing was far more important and effective. In this case, key influencers sent out emails to their engaged audiences that far outperformed the expensive magazine.

Design a Social Media Strategy: In addition to your regular social media activities, you should create a plan for consistent social media campaigns. The aim is to create a buzz and increase awareness for the event. To do this use images, hashtags, handles, videos, and infographics that are easy to share. Create a folder where you organize all of your digital assets. You may be surprised how quickly you can build up a folder of social media content using free and affordable templates online. If your content is sharable you can recruit others to spread the word about the event. If you are posting content regularly, you may find that a specific piece of content outperforms the rest. This may be a sign that you should boost the post and get the message out to more people with advertising. Remember to always engage with your audience. Sometimes it's easy to forget that each person commenting online is a real person. Reply to these event attendees who may become evangelists for your cause. Let them know that they are being heard by responding to comments thoughtfully. When this is done correctly, conversations can be started online that reinforce the value of your event and prompt others to share your content with their online network.

Collaborate with Sponsors/Partners: If you are working with sponsors or partners for the event, synchronize your marketing efforts with theirs. Let your strategies be complementary. At the 2019 StreamGeeks Summit, Amazon AWS became a sponsor. We were very excited to see if their participation could lead to a social media share from one of the massive Amazon accounts. It never happened, but many of our smaller sponsors did share a good deal of our social media content. When appropriate, consider tagging your partners/sponsors in the content you are producing. Many of your partners are eager to get the word out about your event, but not so heavily invested that they would create their own content. By tagging your partners/sponsors they will instantly be notified and prompted to share your post.

Signup on Prominent/Relevant Event Discovery Sites: Make sure your event is listed on the most-used event discovery sites and directories. Our experience using most of these event calendar sites was mediocre at best. If your event appeals to the masses, then it may be more effective. If your event is designed for a niche group of people, save your money and avoid the pay to promote directory sites. You can pay to have your event advertised in the New York Times for a price, but are those readers really interested in your event? Finding the influencer in your niche and working with them to promote your event may prove to be 10X more effective.

Target Audience Aggregators: Audience aggregators are platforms that bring together people with similar characteristics and then sell access to that audience via advertising. Their network could include websites, magazines, social media groups, online forums, and popular hangouts. Working with a company that sells "programmatic advertising" can simplify your life if you can afford the entry level budgets of $10-20k. These services own and operate large networks of websites they can use to put your message in front of their audience. If you do work with a company like this, review their list of online properties and see if their audiences line up with yours.

Networking: Attend events that attract your target audience to meet potential attendees and partners ("20 Creative Event Promotion Ideas to Increase Attendance—Eventbrite," 2018). While promoting the 2019 StreamGeeks Summit, I attended the 2019 TwitchCon show in San. As fate would have it, I met up with multiple key influencers who were interested in the Summit. I attended the event prepared with flyers I could hand out to interested people. One connection led to the next, and before I knew it one gentleman was introducing me to multiple organizations from the NYC area where the event would be held. It's possible 20% of our overall attendees came from one meeting at TwitchCon.

12 PREPARING YOUR EVENT FOR LIVE STREAMING

Venue Considerations:

Venue Layout and Equipment Location

The type of event you are hosting will determine the kind of venue that is most suitable. The venue will affect the way that you are able to set up your event for a live stream. As you select your venue consider where you can set up your recording and streaming equipment. Ideally you should take your live streaming needs into account before choosing a venue. But if you are already locked into an agreement, you can still find ways to work around many difficulties that may arise. Here are the key considerations for your venue ("Venue considerations when livestreaming events," 2018).

- **Obstructions**: Items such as pillars, chandeliers and displays will block line of sight for your production operators and their cameras. Traditionally, obstructions could restrict camera operator movements and limit the number of shots the audience would see. Today most video production professionals are able to use PTZ cameras. These cameras are small and affordable and can be placed in discrete locations around the venue to transport your online audience into your event. For the 2019 StreamGeeks Summit, the production team used six PTZOptics cameras on speaker stands which were located in front of the main conference hall pillars. Back at the production system, the cameras make it easy to see everything going on. Producers can now remotely operate PTZ cameras and move them to various areas on stage with the click of a button.

- **Distractions**: Proximity to areas where there is a lot of movement (restrooms, kitchens, and corridors and doorways) will create distractions that could affect the live stream's audio quality. Audio is king when it comes to video production and any experienced producer will tell you this. It's worth having a dedicated audio producer who can quickly mute any microphone that is causing unwanted noise. The online audience will be very upset if they can't hear what's going on clearly. Online audiences are even more picky than in-person attendees who understand that things can get loud when a crowd of people are moving in the back of the room. Online audiences expect the audio to sound perfect because that is what they have grown accustomed to. Do yourself a favor and hire a dedicated audio production expert, to prevent potential audio issues from occuring.

- **Lighting:** Many rooms are not designed with live streaming in mind, and when lights are dimmed, it can impair the visual quality of your video production. Luckily, most cameras have ways to compensate for low-light situations. As you are planning out your event, consider paying for the lighting package and review your options closely. Good lighting is important to make your video come out well. Cameras and video production software can work some magic with today's latest technology. Color correction is a useful tool in video production software that can be used to match together multiple cameras and compensate for some lighting issues. But even with the best cameras and equipment, nothing can make your production look worse than improper lighting.

PHOTO CREDIT: BERNARD CONNOLLY

- **Staging:** The stage should be high enough to be visible from all camera angles across the room. Consider using tall stable tripods. A popular new technique for live streaming events is the use of speaker stands with dual camera head attachments. Speaker stands are much taller and more stable than traditional camera tripods. You can purchase attachments to allow you to mount PTZ cameras to the top of speaker stands to get your cameras above everyone's head and eye level with people standing on most stages.

- **Audience Seating Arrangement:** Ensure that there is enough room for the crew to move around the event seamlessly. Camera placement can be done very discreetly, and camera views should be placed so there is no obstruction from attendees. Obviously, you want to give your audience easy exit routes if they need to go to the bathroom, but also consider how you will be running cabling. Every venue is different. With PTZ cameras, you can zoom in from far away distances and the audience gets great views of the action. When you pair a zoomed in PTZ camera with a wireless microphone system, you can capture audio and video from 50-100 feet away from the stage. In very large venues, this may mean that you need to put a table area in the crowd, somewhere in the center. For small to medium sized venues, this means that you can place the AV booth at the very back.

- **Location**: The location of power outlets and presence of intrusive art pieces in the room are also important factors to note. It's worth checking with the venue about the power they must provide. Find out exactly how much power your event equipment will need, so you can ask the right questions of your vendors. You can power quite a bit of video production equipment with ethernet cabling. This can be done with a technology called "Power over Ethernet" or "PoE" for short. For example, you may only need power at your main AV booth for your computers, monitors and live streaming gear. But the PTZOptics cameras, for example, have built in PoE, so you can simply run an ethernet cable to each to provide power.

- **Networking**: You should always know the source of your internet access. Most venues today are used to running an ethernet cable wherever it is needed. This ethernet cable comes from the local area network or router which has access to the venue's internet. You should really shy away from using WiFi to live stream because many packets can get lost in translation using WiFi. A hardwired ethernet source is always the best choice. There are cellular bonding solutions that are just as reliable as hard-wired internet from companies like LiveU. LiveU is a company that makes mobile internet streaming solutions that you can use if the venue's internet fails or is unavailable. You can also use LiveU systems to set up a mobile backpack that will allow your team to go behind the scenes with a GoPro style camera.

- **Press Room:** The press room is only necessary for events that attract the media. Even small events can attract media representatives who will hopefully cover your event. Consider creating a free press pass form on your website. It's possible to set up interviews for the press with key people during the event. This may be a great opportunity to capture more quality video content at your event. Consider setting up a backdrop with your event's logo on it where interviews can be recorded. Set up a couple of lights, stools and a video system to capture the interviews. These interviews can be recorded and inserted into your main event's live stream during downtime at your event.

- **Breakout rooms:** Many events offer breakout sessions that allow attendees to partake in smaller classroom style presentations during the event. You can set up these breakout rooms with audio visual equipment to capture each session. These breakout sessions can be offered via on-demand video access later or as their own live stream for virtual ticket holders.

Important Notes for Camera Setup

Here are the key shots you need to have for your video cameras:

- Clear view of the stage/speaker. Consider one wide angle view of the stage and a second camera for zoomed in views of individual speakers.

- A grand view of the audience. A behind the scenes camera view can be used to capture views of the audience during Q&A sessions.

- Close-up of presentation materials. You can capture the video directly from presenters' laptops or capture video from a projector on stage.

- Behind the scenes cameras. "In real life," or IRL cameras generally rove around the event. This is what makes them so powerful. Behind the scenes access areas can be set up to live stream and record additional interviews during the event. Additional recording and streaming systems can be mixed in the cloud into a single presentation streamed to virtual ticket holders.

Video Production Source Ideas

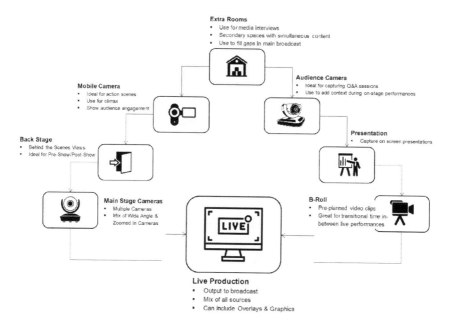

Extra Rooms
- Use for media interviews
- Secondary spaces with simultaneous content
- Use to fill gaps in main broadcast

Mobile Camera
- Ideal for action scenes
- Use for climax
- Show audience engagement

Audience Camera
- Ideal for capturing Q&A sessions
- Use to add context during on-stage performances

Back Stage
- Behind the Scenes Views
- Ideal for Pre-Show/Post-Show

Presentation
- Capture on screen presentations

Main Stage Cameras
- Multiple Cameras
- Mix of Wide Angle & Zoomed In Cameras

B-Roll
- Pre-planned video clips
- Great for transitional time in-between live performances

Live Production
- Output to broadcast
- Mix of all sources
- Can include Overlays & Graphics

Camera placement will of course depend on room size, the equipment you have on hand and the number of rooms your event will have. For events where different sessions will be happening simultaneously, you may need to replicate the camera setup across different rooms. This could also mean that you have multiple streams going on at the same time in order to give online attendees the chance to be in whichever presentation they find more valuable. Your live stream operators will likely have many options to choose from as they produce your event. The more options they have, the better they can produce a high-quality experience for viewers.

Depending on the size of your event you will generally want to have a couple of main stage cameras. If these are PTZ cameras, they can be used to zoom into multiple locations and give audiences a limitless set of views from around the stage. Depending on the level of production quality your event is aiming for, you may want to include cameras that are located behind the scenes or strategically placed to capture the audience. As mentioned earlier, your producers may have access to a mobile roving camera that is ideal for high energy moments during the production. Your production team should also be prepared to show full screen views of presentations as applicable. The team may also be prepared to show "B-Roll" which is an industry term for short video clips. You can prepare video clips to fill the void between various segments of your production or use b-roll to enhance various live moments. Your production may even be able to connect to a separate production system connected to the network. This could be ideal for down-time during the mainstream which can switch to a stream from a separate room.

For the 2019 StreamGeeks Summit, there was only one main online live stream going on, even though there were breakout sessions during the conference. These breakout sessions were sold as part of the premium access tickets to be made available after the conference. This breakout room was set up like a classroom with tables and chairs organized into a "U" shape. In this room, there was a PTZOptics producer kit set up with a two-microphone system. One camera was a PTZOptics 12X-SDI placed on a tripod to capture the video of the presenter. There was also a wireless microphone for the presenter and a microphone for the audience. During each presentation, someone was available to press the record button. When you are dealing with lots of recordings it's important to think about video storage and hard drive space. Here is a simple chart of video resolutions and bitrates you can use to determine your video quality settings for recordings.

Resolution	Frame Rate	Bitrate	Format	File Size (60 min)
1280x720	30fps	8Mbps	mp4	2 GB
1920x1080	30fps	8Mbps	mp4	4 GB
4K	30fps	8Mbps	mp4	6 GB
1280x720	30fps	16Mbps	mp4	4 GB
1920x1080	30fps	16Mbps	mp4	8 GB
4K	30fps	16Mbps	mp4	12 GB
1280x720	60fps	8Mbps	mp4	4 GB
1920x1080	60fps	8Mbps	mp4	8 GB
4K	60fps	8Mbps	mp4	12 GB

Files sizes may vary based on the system used. Changing the file format will impact files size significantly.

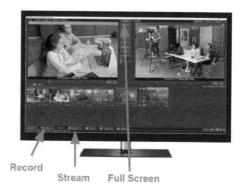

Record

Stream   Full Screen

Most YouTube videos recorded in Full HD (1920x1080p) are played back to viewers between 0-12 Mbps depending on available bandwidth. The higher that your bitrate is, the higher quality your video recordings will be. Bitrate is a term used to describe the transfer of data, and therefore you will see it referenced for file recording and streaming. When Bitrates are used for recording, you are determining the quality (and size) of your recordings. When Bitrates are used for streaming, this refers to the quality of your live stream. Once a file has been recorded, the bits are referred to as bytes. For example, you can live stream at 2Mbps. If you record the live stream at 8 Mbps for 60 minutes you will have a file size of 2 Gigabytes.

Equation for File Size Calculation:

Frame Rate X Bitrate X Size of Frames (Bitrate X Resolution) X Time = File Size

Bitrate and framerate are the main determining factors for file size. You can use a video file size calculator online to quickly determine the size of your video recordings and the bandwidth needed for your live streams. For basic presentation recordings you can get away with a low bit rate of 3-6 Mbps. For beautiful events with lots of lights and color, consider upping your bitrate to capture that depth between 20-100 Mbps. If your event is on par with a Hollywood film, you could perhaps use absolutely no compression which creates massive files. Just keep in mind the length your videos will be, and the amount of hard drive space required to capture that video given the bitrate, framerate and file format you choose. For most events, 30 frames per second is fine. In fact, using 60 frames per second can look unnatural fo many scenarios. If you are capturing an event with fast moving objects such as dancers or sports, you can consider using 60 frames per second. High frame rate events require more storage for recordings and bandwidth for live streaming.

Internet Connection Types

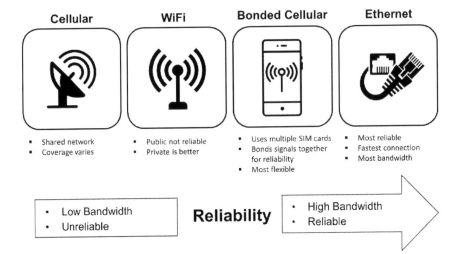

Cellular	WiFi	Bonded Cellular	Ethernet
• Shared network • Coverage varies	• Public not reliable • Private is better	• Uses multiple SIM cards • Bonds signals together for reliability • Most flexible	• Most reliable • Fastest connection • Most bandwidth

• Low Bandwidth • Unreliable	**Reliability**	• High Bandwidth • Reliable

Internet Bandwidth & Streaming

The internet is another highly critical factor for your live stream. Without it you will not have a live stream at all. And even if you do have an internet connection, if there is not enough available bandwidth, your broadcast can be choppy or get disconnected. The quality of your connection can serve up a frustrating experience for viewers and ruin all of your hard work. There are four main internet connection options, and each has its own characteristics ("How to live stream an event," 2019).

- <u>Cellular Network (3G/4G)</u>: This is a shared cellular network that you can use along with hundreds of people who attend the event, as well as others in the vicinity. Streaming on a cellular network is prone to failures and packet loss. Yet there are ways to make it usable. LiveU is a company that has developed cellular-bonding solutions that bridge together multiple SIM cards to create a reliable streaming system that can broadcast your event wirelessly. The LiveU solo, for example, allows you to connect to the rooms WiFi, ethernet, and two cellular connections to create one super reliable connection. Many professional live streamers have been burned by the cellular connection available or the venue's available internet. Cellular bonding solutions allow you to bring high quality bandwidth almost anywhere. Once 5G is available, live streaming on a cellular connection will become even more reliable.

- Local Wi-Fi: Wi-Fi is preferred to cellular connection. Be wary public Wi-Fi. Public Wi-Fi that the event venue offers can generally be very slow. This connection again may be shared by many other users. Most modern conferences will offer attendees access to Wi-Fi. Wi-Fi is generally good for non-critical web-browsing. But be wary of relying on Wi-Fi for your live streaming.

- Local Ethernet Connection: A hard-wired ethernet connection is the recommended connection type for many reasons. This type of connectivity offers a stable connection for a high-quality broadcast assuming the internet access is good enough. With a hard-wired ethernet connection you have the lowest likelihood of packets being dropped during your live stream.

- Checking Bandwidth: The easiest way to quickly check your bandwidth is to Google "Speed Test". Google will deliver a speed check directly through the search engine. Remember that the download speed is just for requesting information from the internet. You want to be checking the upload speeds for live streaming.

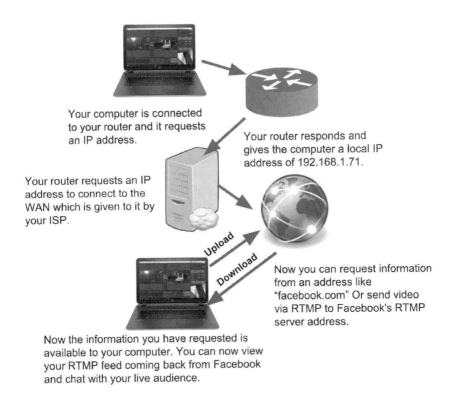

Your computer is connected to your router and it requests an IP address.

Your router responds and gives the computer a local IP address of 192.168.1.71.

Your router requests an IP address to connect to the WAN which is given to it by your ISP.

Upload
Download

Now you can request information from an address like "facebook.com" Or send video via RTMP to Facebook's RTMP server address.

Now the information you have requested is available to your computer. You can now view your RTMP feed coming back from Facebook and chat with your live audience.

Bandwidth is measured in bits and the word "bandwidth" is used to describe the maximum data transfer rate of your internet connection. When you measure this speed, you are measuring megabits as they relate to time. One megabit = 1,000 kilobits and generally, you will talk about megabits per second which is the amount of data you can stream every second. Your internet connection is measured in upload and download speeds. Megabits are used to measure the size of the bandwidth pipeline between your computer and the internet.

Think about your live stream resolution as the size of your canvas like a painting. The bitrate that you select is the amount of data that is used to fill that canvas. Therefore, you can have a high-quality 1080p stream with a bit rate of 6 Mbps, or you can have a low-quality 1080p stream with a bit rate of just 2 Mbps. New reports from Akamai show that most people watching 1080p video find that 6Mbps looks like excellent quality (O'Halloran, 2018).

Resolution	Pixel Count	Frame Rate	Quality	Bandwidth
4K 30fps	3840x2160	30fps	High	30Mbps
4K 30fps	3840x2160	30fps	Medium	20Mbps
4K 30fps	3840x2160	30fps	Low	10Mbps
1080p60fps	1920x1080	60fps	High	12Mbps
1080p60fps	1920x1080	60fps	Medium	9Mbps
1080p60fps	1920x1080	60fps	Low	6Mbps
1080p30fps	1920x1080	30fps	High	6Mbps
1080p30fps	1920x1080	30fps	Medium	4.5Mbps
1080p30fps	1920x1080	30fps	Low	3Mbps
720p30fps	1280x720	30fps	High	3.5Mbps
720p30fps	1280x720	30fps	Medium	2.5Mbps
720p30fps	1280x720	30fps	Low	1.5Mbps

The chart above displays various bandwidth choices you will have for your live streams. Using this chart and your available uploads speeds, you should be able to map out the number and quality of live streams your internet connection can support. You may want to have multiple streams available during your event which can be switched in the cloud. Or you may want to have one main live stream being sent to a private CDN and others that are periodically sent to social media.

A general rule of thumb says that you should only use half of your available upload speeds for live streaming (download speeds don't help with live streaming). Therefore, if you have 10 Mbps of available upload speed, you should only be live streaming with 5 Mbps. This leaves headroom for your upload speeds to protect the quality which can be affected by fluctuations in the internet connection. These fluctuations happen all the time and they can cause interference with your stream's consistency.

Keep in mind that most live streaming software will now allow you to live stream to multiple locations at the same time. A new update to vMix, for example, allows users to toggle on and off three unique destinations. So, you may have a choice between live streaming a single high-quality video stream, or multiple live streams of lesser quality. For example, if you have 10 Mbps of upload speed, you may create a 3 Mbps stream to YouTube and a 2Mbps stream to Facebook. If you are concerned about creating a single high-quality stream, then you would only stream to YouTube using 5Mbps. Keep in mind that you can always record an incredibly high-quality recording to your local hard drive, and post it online after the event.

Adaptive Bit Rates

Today most CDNs are providing something called "adaptive bitrate streaming." This technology takes the best quality stream you send and breaks it down into smaller resolutions and bitrates for viewers with lower internet speeds to view in a reliable stream. CDNs such as YouTube and Facebook will use Adaptive Bitrate Streaming to optimize the video quality your viewers receive based on their available internet access. This further supports the need to stream in the highest quality possible to allow the CDN to make the best choices for viewers on their platform. Some CDN's also call this process "Live Cloud Encoding."

Audio Considerations

Sound is massively important for the success of your live streams. If people cannot hear the speakers at your event or the reactions from the audience, they may abandon the broadcast halfway and give you a bad review. For most events, even if your video is not HD quality, viewers are willing to forgive that, if the sound is understandable. On the other hand, good video quality will not make up for poor sound. The key things to keep in mind for ensuring that sound is being captured from appropriately are below.

- **Microphone Placement**: The audio quality for your event is very dependent on the microphone placement for each area/speaker. There are many different types of microphones and many speakers do not know how to use each microphone type properly. The most trust-worthy type of microphone is a headset microphone. These microphones slip behind the ear of a speaker and they stay in place next to the speaker's mouth no matter what the speaker is doing. Lapel microphones are perhaps the second best, because they generally stay in place for most speakers. Lapel microphones are prone to many issues including the ruffling of shirts and misplacement. The reason why lapel microphones are popular is because of how easy they are to simply clip on to a shirt. Handheld microphones are great for on-the-fly use. But they are also error prone because most speakers don't think about how close the microphone needs to be to their mouths for proper pickup. Shotgun microphones can be used to capture large areas, but they pick up a lot of ambient noise. Therefore, these types of microphones should be used for just that, picking up ambient noise. Ambient noise is only nice to have when you need it and it should be monitored and muted when it does not add to the viewer experience. With all these various types of microphones, it's very important to have an audio person managing the levels on each. A good audio engineer will label each input on their audio mixer and listen to the entire mix with headphones. A decent pair of headphones are always important to mixing the audio for live events.

- **In room audio**: There are essentially two audio mixes that are produced for most events. One is the in-room audio and one is for the live stream audio. The in-room audio experience is designed for the in-person event attendees and it may be slightly different than the live stream audio. While you may use the same microphones for both audio mixes, when you are live streaming you need to consider different issues such as copyright and compression. For example, you may have the radio playing during your event between speakers. If your live stream is somehow capturing the audio from the radio, Facebook or YouTube may shut down the live stream or flag the broadcast due to a copyright violation. You will not have this issue with private CDNs, but you would still be breaking the law, if you do not have the appropriate licenses for music you are broadcasting. You can of course visit websites with large copy-right free music collections online to find legal music to broadcast.

- **Troubleshooting Audio**: Possible issues with the in-room audio experience include audio that is too loud, too quiet and/or too distorted. Proper placement of speakers and microphones will be essential to any audio system. Placing a microphone in front of a speaker will create feedback. Placing the speakers in front of the microphones can generally eliminate that issue. If issues occur as you are testing out your audio system, the audio engineer will start troubleshooting by muting inputs on your audio mixer. Once you have figured out which microphone inputs are causing the issue, you can work on the placement. Don't wait until the last minute to test your audio system. You should start by testing your in-room audio and then follow that by testing the live production system audio.

- **Music**: You will likely be playing some music during your event. You should always obtain the proper licensing for playing this music for your in-person audience and your online audience. Just because you have obtained the proper licensing for playing music at your event doesn't mean you can also broadcast that music online. When you are playing music in your venue you can generally mute all your microphones to avoid feedback. When you are playing music for your live stream audience, it can be totally different from the in-room event music. You should always have one set of headphones for your audio mixer and one set for your live streaming computer. Always make sure that you are not using copyrighted music on your live stream because you can capture audio from sources like the radio by mistake. AudioBlocks.com is a great website with many low cost music you can obtain licensing to broadcast with.

- **Capturing Audio for Streaming**: Your live streaming computer will have its own audio mix that will be sent to your live viewers. Most live streaming systems use a USB audio interface which plugs directly into a live streaming computer via USB and captures the audio from the main audio mixer via an audio output. Most audio mixers feature multiple audio outputs that can be used with XLR or ¼" audio cables to bring that audio into your USB audio interface.

- **Audio Sync**: The final test you should perform is an audio sync test. It's very common to have a short time delay between the cameras and the audio system. This can easily be adjusted with almost any video production software by adding a little bit of delay to your audio. You can test this by having someone speak in a microphone and count to five. Have this person use their fingers to visually signal the number they are saying "one, two, three, four, five." Watch their mouth and fingers to determine if there is a noticeable delay. If there is a noticeable delay simply add delay to the audio in increments of 25 milliseconds. Audio is almost always transmitted faster than video because the bitrate is much smaller and easier to process. The StreamGeeks have a great tool called the

Audio Video Sync tool you can download from our website to get this process perfect every time.

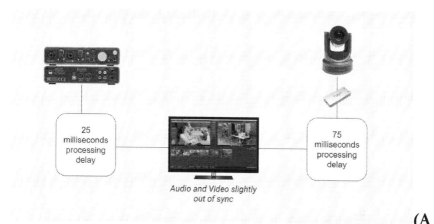

(Adding 50 milliseconds of audio delay will fix this system)

Readying Your Content For Virtual Audiences

All live streams are not created equal, but the quality of the final product does not have to depend on how much money you spend. So much of the live viewer experience you deliver depends on how much attention is given to the project. Apart from the event venue and equipment, another important variable is the event speakers. The event speakers and/or performers are a factor that you can never be 100% in control over. To ensure your online audience gets the best quality for their money, it is important to have pre-event meetings with your talent in order to work out the little details that affect online presentation quality.

- Speakers should be capable of making a good visual presentation. You can consider having speakers provide short video introduction clips that you can play on the live stream before they arrive on stage. If possible, you should have an HD screen capture of their presentation that can be in your live stream. You can do this with a picture in picture set up.

Video Production Presentation Layout Styles

Full Screen

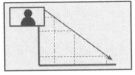

Picture in Picture #1

Picture in Picture #2

- Presentation materials should be previewed to make sure they are clearly visible and will be easily understood by all audiences. An easy way to capture slides from a laptop over the network is called NDI scan converter. You can use NDI scan converter on most Windows and Mac computers to send a video feed of the presentation over your network. NDI works with video production software such as vMix, Wirecast, xSplit, OBS and many more. You can also use traditional HDMI to USB capture cards. With a capture card you can use an HDMI output from the presentation laptop and convert it to USB for the live streaming computer to use.

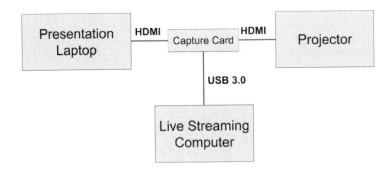

- Speakers should be comfortable addressing the online audience directly and responding to their questions. If you have a chat room moderator on staff, they can use a microphone to voice questions from the online audience.

- Make event materials accessible and easy to download for online attendees. If your speakers have presentations, ask if they can be shared online. This is especially helpful if you are selling on-demand access to the speaker's recorded video. Consider using an online education website like Udemy for hosting your event's content. Udemy, for example, allows content creators to charge up to $200 per course. Udemy has a great marketplace for selling online video courses and it was used to deliver the StreamGeeks Summit's premium video tickets. On a platform like this you can upload files for each recorded video. Consider uploading the speaker's presentation documents here to supplement the video recordings.

- Translate presentations that are to be included with translated broadcasts. If you are planning multiple broadcasts in various languages, you should prepare translated presentations as well. Each live streaming computer that is managing the translated broadcasts can have their own copies of the translated materials. While some audio-visual sources may be shared such as the cameras, the translated presentations should be unique for each language.

Live Streaming Equipment

You do not need expensive equipment to do a live stream and monetize it. There are three common equipment set-ups you can have for a live stream. There are mobile systems, laptop-based systems and professional systems.

Mobile Set-Up: $0 - $1,500

Requirements:

- Smartphone or tablet

- Stable internet

- Content Delivery Network with paywall or user gate

- Microphone systems (wireless optional)

- Tripod & zoom lens (optional)

- Extra phone battery (optional)

Laptop Set-Up: $1,500 - $10.000

Requirements:

- Windows PC (i5 or higher) or Macbook

- Encoder software installed on laptop (OBS, Wirecast, vMix)

- Simple IP network (used to capture slides from presenter's laptop)

- 2 HD cameras (camcorders or PTZ cameras)

- Content Delivery Network with a paywall

- Video capture devices (HDMI or SDI to USB)

- Stable internet or cellular bonding system

- Audio mixer and USB audio interface

- Camera tripods (Speaker stands are better)

- Headsets/mics/comms

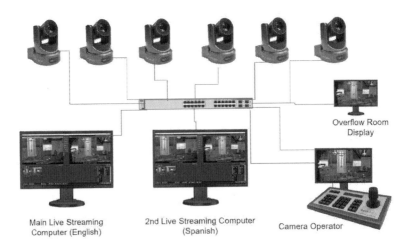

94

Pro Set-Up: $10,000 and over
Requirements:

- 3+ Professional level PTZ cameras with HD output via HDMI or SDI

- An IP network that delivers power to PoE devices (Power over Ethernet)

- Professional Microphones (Table mics, boom mics, etc)

- Multiple streaming computers (one for each stream, additional computers for social media management and graphics)

- Video editing software (live to tape editing and rendering for on-demand videos)

- Extensive cabling

- Encoding hardware (cellular bonding system)

- Lighting

- Monitors (Confidence monitors for speakers)

- Projector (In-room projection for presentations)

- Stable internet

- Professional crew

13 MINDFUL VIDEO PRODUCTION

It's now time to review how to properly produce a show from the perspective of the technical director. An event production is essentially an orchestrated process of capturing the show's content with your audiovisual equipment. In order to do this, the technical director must make decisions about how and when to transition between the available video and audio sources. The goal of a good technical director is to produce a cohesive storyline. As you transition between one scene to the next, it's important to think about the viewer's experience as they follow along with your production. Choosing the appropriate transition moments and using the correct transition type will be essential in capturing your audience's attention and making the technology flow seamlessly.

Producers can use transition effects to complement their production capabilities. A good transition seamlessly leads the audience through one scene to the next. The best transition is one that keeps the audience captivated by the content. In a perfect world, the transition happens as if the viewer naturally selected it. In order to do this, your production should flow in a way that feels natural to viewers. Be careful not to use fancy transitions that could take away from the main message of your content. Below you will see the four most popular transitions used in video production. In order of popularity, these would be the cut, the fade, the fade to black and the stinger transition effects.

Type	How Commonly Used
Cut	90% of the time
Fade	<5%
Other/Stinger	<5%

You will notice that there are quite a few options in your video production software when it comes to video transition effects. The most used video transition is a cut. The cut simply switches two video sources with a direct cut that does not use any special effects. The cut should be used for transitioning between most of your prepared content. The cut is perfect for transitioning between two live camera angles in the same scene. When you are cutting between multiple camera angles that you have in one scene, it is important to think about the camera angles. Jumping to too many different camera angles too quickly could be disorienting for your viewers. A good technical director will visualize the camera angles that they have available and move through them in a natural order. You should try to arrange your camera angles so that you can reveal additional details as they become more important to the story. If you have a pan, tilt and zoom camera that can capture multiple angles during a single production, consider switching back and forth between close up angles and your available wide-angle shots. You don't want to cut to a camera angle that is more than 45 degrees away from your current camera angle. In this way, you can switch between multiple cameras in an arc to finally reach a camera that may show a side or behind the scenes camera angle.

Interview diagram #1

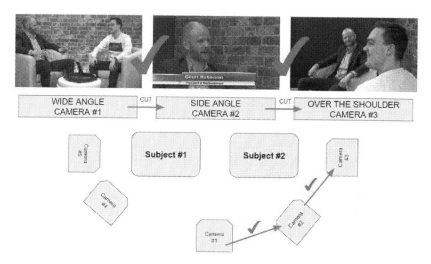

To study these production techniques, review the example of a two-person interview. When you are producing an interview like this, it's a good idea to start with a wide angle shot that displays all of your subjects in the same shot. This is your central shot that establishes placement for the viewers in the scene that they are watching. The cut transition can then be used to enhance the viewer's perspective of each person as they take turns talking. A transition like a fade or a stinger would look unnatural for this type of production. The cut makes the camera switching feel natural and unnoticeable because it happens in the blink of an eye. Each transition should be timed to flow with the conversation your subjects are having.

Interview diagram #2

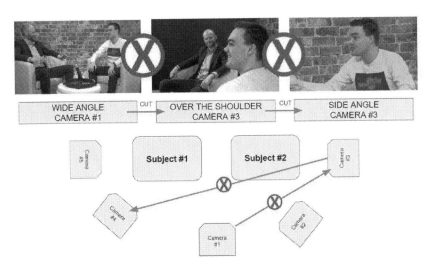

As you can see in the production workflow of the interview diagram #1, the producer has selected to move between the camera cuts that are sequential around the arc of camera options moving counterclockwise. Interview diagram #2 shows a sequence of transitions that do not follow sequential movements around the camera inputs that are available and beyond the 45-degree rule from the last camera angle. Using these types of "jumpy cuts" could be disorienting for viewers. Remember that all rules are meant to be broken, and every camera setup is different. Use your instincts and create a production that makes sense for the story you want to tell.

Show Flow Examples

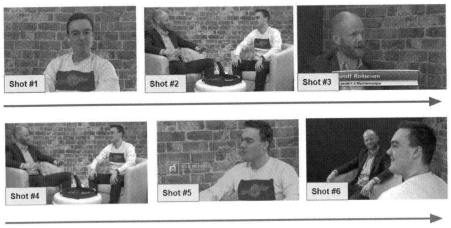

The crossfade transition is perhaps the second most popular transition in live video production. You will notice that they are used much less frequently than the cut, but they are often given prime real estate in many production systems. Crossfade transitions can produce beautiful artistic visual effects. The crossfade should be used in this way to enhance your production. Crossfades are used frequently during musical performances such as the national anthem performed just before a sports event. You will notice the crossfade is used when the cameras switch between a close up of a singer and a wide panning shot of a crowd. You will notice great crossfade transitions that feature the American flag slowly fading into a crowd of singing sports fans.

Crossfade used during national anthem

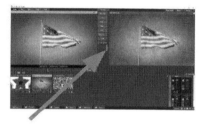

Crossfade t-bar position at 50%. **Crossfade t-bar position at 90%.**

If you have an artistic shot prepared for your next video production project, the crossfade may be the most appropriate transition to use. If you have a pan, tilt and zoom camera, try transitioning with the crossfade when the camera is in between a slow pan. Many professional broadcast studios use a physical T-bar to create custom cross-fade transitions between multiple video inputs. Use this transition sparingly and note that crossfades may look pixelated in low bitrate bandwidth streams.

The fade to black, sometimes shortened to just "FTB", is perhaps the next most used video transition. You can fade to black and fade from black to notify the beginning or the end of your production. This type of video transition clearly demonstrates the nonverbal communication power you have as a producer. If you can time your fade to black with the ending points of an audio track, you will really be doing great. Hopefully, your audio director will work in sync and fade the audio track for you as the video fades to black.

Finally, the stinger transition is an animated transition that everybody has grown to love. The effect combines a transparent video animation that evolves into a full screen overlay which is timed with a cut transition. When your stinger video animation starts playing on top of your current video, you can program your production software to cut to your preview input exactly when the video completely covers up the current scene. The stinger effect has been made popular by sports broadcasters who use the effect to notify the audience of a scene change. In this way, sports broadcasters have trained their audience to expect a stinger transition when an instant replay or prepared video screen is coming up. Really fancy stinger video animations often include perfectly timed audio which has audio with lots of "whooshes" and "pops" perfectly timed to give the animation a realistic effect. Remember that most viewers have never heard of a "stinger effect" yet the nonverbal connection that is made to the audience takes effect immediately.

14 INNOVATIONS IN VIDEO CONFERENCING, LIVE STREAMING AND CONTENT DELIVERY

Video communications and content delivery technologies have gone through an amazing period of innovation and change over the past decade. Video conferencing technology has moved to the cloud allowing anyone, almost anywhere, to connect and communicate with an ease. Live video streaming has made its way into social media putting a "go live" button into the hands of billions of users. This democratization of technology has led to all kinds of new use cases bubbling to the surface where only the strongest and most captivating ideas survive. Throughout this process companies such as Twitch, Facebook, Zoom Video Conferencing, vMix, Wirecast, and NewTek have experienced explosive growth by listening to customers and scaling their offerings to match growing market requirements.

In this chapter, you can learn about the latest new innovations in live streaming, video conferencing and content delivery that will make your events more productive. Event planners should understand the latest features in live streaming, video conferencing, social media, and collaboration software in order to best design immersive experiences for online attendees. To begin your thinking about these software solutions, first think about your event in the public eye. Is your event going to be public, private, or a mix of both?

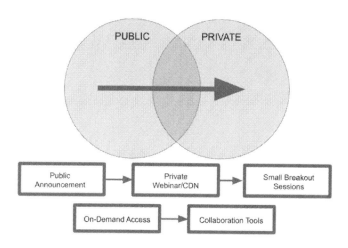

Social media websites are the ideal destinations for purely public events, because they offer the largest amount of exposure and shareability. Event planners may require events to be held in a private space where only paying customers have access. Private events can leverage video conferences and webinars that require unique registration lists. Hosting a private webinar or video conference is an easy way for event planners to hold private presentations that offer user engagement tools. For example, a Zoom Webinar can host an online event with up to 100 interactive video participants and up to 10,000 view only participants. For many event planners, this is plenty of space for holding a private virtual event. Zoom offers a cloud-based dashboard that provides event managers a single place to manage registrations and integrations with existing CRM systems. This webinar system, and most others in the market, offer live Q&A, polling, attendees can raise their hands, and there's even a new attention indication feature. For event planners, who want to easily monetize their webinars, Zoom offers a PayPal integration through service called Zapier.

One of the most innovative new features that Zoom announced at the 2019 Zoomtopia conference is live translations. Zoom has supported automatic video transcriptions since 2017, which is a feature that provides speech to text file processing in the cloud. The new translation feature provides live translators who can translate your conference in real time and deliver the translated audio to groups of participants around the world. This new feature allows meeting participants to select their meeting language of choice, from a list of available live interpreters. Meeting participants will hear the interpreters at 80% audio levels and the original speaker at 20%.

Live Broadcast Translation

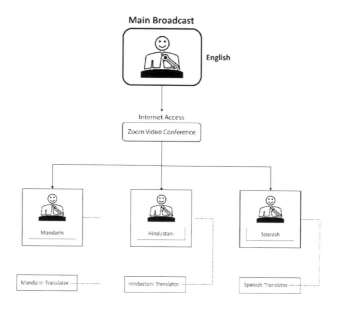

Innovations in the video conferencing industry can be used to complement events in many ways. While software like Zoom was not designed for multi-camera video productions, it's quite easy to capture an events video production system output and use it with Zoom. The easiest way to capture a video production software and bring it into a video conferencing software is through a device called an HDMI to USB capture card. You can simply take the HDMI video/audio output from a production system and bring that video direction into a software like Zoom via the USB webcam and audio inputs.

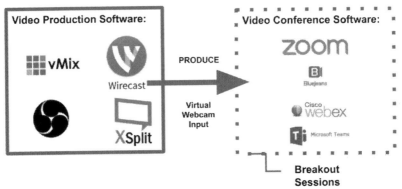

Innovation in the video production industry has made live streaming and audience engagement easier and more interactive. A company called vMix has developed a tool called vMix social which can now integrate with Facebook, YouTube, Twitch, Twitter, and IRC to manage comments that can be moderated and displayed up on screen. The software provides a simple dashboard for curated social media comments and quickly selecting the messages that can be automatically overlaid on top of the broadcast. Another powerful feature that makes events more interactive is called data sources. This feature allows broadcasters to integrate data sources directly into on-screen titles. Information sources can include Google Sheets, Excel, RSS, XML, Text and more. While this feature may sound overly technical, here is a simple example. Your live production is going on and there is a title which is automatically updated with timely information via a Google Sheet. The event manager only needs to enter information directly into a Google Sheet on their laptop or smartphone to have direct access to the information being displayed on the live stream. Here is another example. A non-profit is hosting a live fundraising event, where they are accepting donations via YouTube Super Chat. The super chats (live donations), are being logged in a Google Sheet which is automatically displaying the latest supporters of the project in-real time on the live stream.

Ideas for Successful Video Production

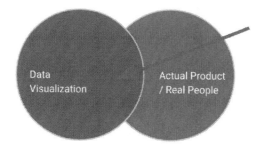

Data visualization and collaboration can help educational events find the happy medium between education and entertainment. Charts, graphs and PowerPoint presentations are great but try striking a balance between data and real-life representations of the data is where broadcasters can capture audience attention. If you have an app, zoom into the app and share the latest feature. If you sell a product, zoom into the product and share it's look and feel. If you can make your presentation entertaining it will increase viewer retention. Consider ways to strike a balance between information and entertainment.

Another amazing new technology in the video production space is IP video. A particularly innovative new video production standard is called the NewTek NDI. This technology makes sending and receiving high quality video sources over the local area network incredibly easy. Software like Wirecast, OBS, vMix, Livestream Studio, and many more all support this standard. NDI allows video production companies create television quality productions on budgets that are extremely low. Along with IP video production, IP connectivity for devices like PTZ cameras is now allowing smaller teams of producers to do more for large events. PTZOptics cameras for example, support the NewTek NDI and have direct PTZ camera control integrations with software such as vMix, Wirecast, OBS, Livestream Studio and NewTek TriCasters. In this way, event managers can use a single ethernet cable to power up a camera (via PoE), receive HD video, and control a PTZ camera.

Note: To learn more about the NewTek NDI or PTZOptics cameras consider taking on my free courses available on Udemy.

On the content delivery network side, many new innovations are starting to transform what is possible for event managers. Many CDN's are now allowing broadcasters the ability to monetize their live streams by overlaying instant ads on top of the live video streams. For example, your favorite soccer player makes an amazing goal. At this moment, broadcasters are able to overlay a link for where to buy the players jersey directly on top of the video player. Twitch is a company taking full advantage of the concept with their feature called "Twitch Extensions." Twitch extensions are a library of tools that broadcasters can use to overlay interactive elements on top of their video players. An example of this in esports, is an interactive button that shows additional information about the video game currently being played. For video games that support this integration, viewers can interact with live elements of the game, such as the players inventory. Another example of this developed by PTZOptics, is a behind the scenes camera control extension that gives the audience control of a PTZ camera. This is currently being used by high profile artists who can set up a camera backstage and charge live viewers for the capability of controlling the audience view inside of an engaging space.

Keeping up with the latest innovations for live streaming, video conferencing and content delivery is what the StreamGeeks are all about. Because this information is constantly changing, I highly recommend joining the StreamGeeks Facebook Group and following our team on social media.

15 PUTTING THE FUN BACK IN FUNDRAISING

Far gone are the dull fundraisers of the past, where audiences viewed people manning a bank of telephones with one host explaining the non-profit's mission. Today, fundraising can be fresh, fun and even a little bit silly! With bubble machines, confetti cannons, and other interactive tools, audiences can be inspired to share fundraisers with their friends and family, extending the reach of your non-profit.

The fundraiser here was anything but typical. It was set up to use YouTube's SuperChat feature, which allowed viewers to make donations and be entertained simultaneously. Using SuperChat with a service called IFTTT, the StreamGeeks were able to trigger devices on the live stream when donations were made. The StreamGeeks used a balloon machine, a bubble machine, confetti cannons and much more to engage live viewers and thank them for their donations. This is a perfect example of how small non-profits can make a big impact with live streaming online.

The picture above shows the live fundraiser on YouTube in action. StreamGeeks used IFTTT to set up Super Chat donations to do various activities:

- $1 - $1.99 donation triggered a colored balloon blown up
- $2 - $4.99 donation triggered an emoji balloon blown up
- $5 - $9.99 donation triggered a Star Wars balloon blown up
- $10 - $19.99 donation triggered a bubble machine use

- $10 - $49.99 donation triggered a confetti cannon blast
- $50 - $99.99 donation triggered a confetti cannon blast and a bubble machine use
- $100 donation triggered a multi-camera confetti cannon slow-mo

Non-profit organizations raised $120 million dollars on Facebook during the 24 hours of Giving Tuesday on December 3rd. Over 1.1 million people created fundraisers or donated to help 97,000 charitable organizations around the world. Social media websites like Facebook have made starting a fundraising campaign easier than ever before. Users can quickly select a non-profit organization, determine why they are raising money, set a goal and choose a timeframe - all from a smartphone (Facebook, 2019).

Social media sharing has vastly improved fundraising capabilities for non-profits over the past decade. The Non-Profit Source says that "55% of people who engage with nonprofits on social media end up taking some sort of action" and "18% of donors worldwide have given through Facebook fundraising tools." Another striking example of social sharing is the fact that "84% of Facebook users share to show their support for a cause and highlight issues that are important to them." With so much positive energy available online to support non-profits, it's no wonder why live streaming fundraisers on social media have become so popular (Non-Profit Source, 2019).

Facebook	YouTube
• Best shareability • Easiest to work with • Easiest to to promote	• Most advanced features • Longest video shelf life • Most videos watched by potential donors

Many non-profits host exclusive events with the intent to sell tickets to raise money for their organizations. Selling virtual tickets to these events allow non-profits to expand their reach and lower the cost of entry. In 2018, the StreamGeeks worked with the local Chester County Historical Society to live-stream its annual Halloween Ball. The StreamGeeks team used the LiveU Solo, which provides high-quality internet access from anywhere in the event. This device was hidden in a backpack, and our team walked around with a selfie stick taking live viewers through the event.

The most important aspect of live streaming is engaging online viewers. If you are a non-profit hoping to use live streaming for fundraising the first thing to consider is your presentation. As a non-profit with little experience live streaming, you shouldn't worry about having a small number of social media followers. When you start live streaming you may have no audience at all. With small audiences, it can be difficult to get the most important value out of live streaming, which is real-time engagement.

Working hard on your storytelling capabilities is an important start in engaging audiences. Set up an interesting premise for your fundraiser and think about how the live audience engagement can enhance your storyline. Throw out anything in your presentation that is boring: live video needs to be exciting. Save the boring details for some other step in your list of fundraising goals. Start by presenting your non-profit with a story that is worthy of viewer attention. Once you have your audience's attention, it's time to hone in on their focus. What has your organization done with the money that you have raised in the past? What will your organization be able to do with the money that you are attempting to raise now?

Using multiple cameras, creative slides, and anything that you have available to gain viewer focus and passive participation should be used. Passive participation is what leads to active participation, which may come through viewer chat messages or post engagements. As you are engaging with your audience you want to learn how to educate and entertain at the same time. If you can educate your audience while keeping them entertained, you can get a reaction out of them. Reactions can create desire, commitment and even change viewers' thinking on various subjects. During a fundraiser, you are hoping to inspire the viewers' desire to help your cause. The reaction you are trying to create is a donation.

Ultimately, you want to transform your audience and give them a new aspiration for something you are passionate about. Sound like a lot? To simplify the steps above think about your presentations and give them a clear beginning, middle and an end. Give your presentations a little drama and plan out a climax. Audiences love climaxes, and this is where the most engagement will occur. A perfect mini climax is a donation that comes in from the audience. You can extend this moment by ringing a bell, sharing the donor's information or even having a confetti cannon go off. Once you have reached your fundraising goals, this is the event's planned climax. Extend your fundraising capabilities from here with a planned exit.

It's a lot to juggle for a single person so think about having a team in place for live streaming a fundraiser. It takes a lot of practice, and it doesn't always go as planned. Learn how to connect with audiences using a regular live stream first. Build up your experiences with a weekly show or a monthly live stream. Once you are ready you can create an amazing fundraiser for something you and your team are passionate about.

16 WHAT'S NEXT?

It's exciting to see how quickly the events industry is growing. In an increasingly interconnected world, humans still crave in-person experiences that can break through the clutter of our media saturated lives. The statistics show consumers are more willing than ever before to pay for experiences that lift them from their normal lives and engage them in new and exciting ways. As the events industry continues to grow, a very real opportunity continues to grow for virtual experiences that transport audiences into events that they are unable to attend in person. Event planners can use the same deep thinking that goes into planning immersive experiences and apply new technologies that can deliver audio visuals to online audiences. When done correctly, with the proper attention to detail, event managers can expand their audiences internationally in ways that audiences are only just beginning to gain a glimpse into.

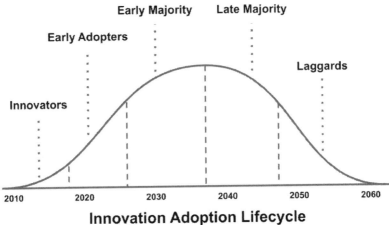

Innovation Adoption Lifecycle

Learning is a process, and this book has been written for readers who want to uncover opportunities for event planning in the modern age. As of early 2020, there could not be a more important time in history for events to modernize their value delivery. Consumers are adapting to changing economics, healthcare, technology and habits at a time when social media and video communications are starting to mature and scale. If you are reading this book, you are an innovator and an early adopter of event management innovation in the digital age. Use the ideas you have generated from reading this book and pair them with your team's creativity. Use your status as an early adopter to your advantage and get out ahead of your competition.

If you have any questions along your journey of implementing a virtual ticket program, consider reaching out to the StreamGeeks on Facebook. We have set up a Facebook group dedicated to event managers who are implementing virtual tickets into their experiences called "The Virtual Ticket for Event Managers." Our team is active on social media and we always love to see what innovative people are doing with live streaming around the world.

Sincerely,

Paul Richards
Chief Streaming Officer
StreamGeeks
Email: paul.richards@streamgeeks.us

GLOSSARY OF TERMS

3.5mm Audio Cable - Male to male stereo cable, common in standard audio uses.

4K - A high definition resolution option (3840 x 2160 pixels or 4096 x 2160 pixels)

16:9 [16x9] - Aspect ratio of 9 units of height and 16 units of width. Used to describe standard HDTV, Full HD, non-HD digital television and analog widescreen television.

API [Application Program Interface]- A streaming API is a set of data a social media network uses to transmit on the web in real time. Going live directly from YouTube or Facebook uses their API.

Bandwidth - Bandwidth is measured in bits and the word "bandwidth" is used to describe the maximum data transfer rate.

Bitrate – Bitrates are used to select the data transfer size of your live stream. This is the number of bits per second that can be transmitted along a digital network.

Broadcasting - The distribution of audio or video content to a dispersed audience via any electronic mass communications medium.

Broadcast Frame Rates - Used to describe how many frames per second are captured in broadcasting. Common frame rates in broadcast include **29.97fps and 59.97 fps**.

Capture Card - A device with inputs and outputs that allow a camera to connect to a computer.

Chroma Key - A video effect that allows you to layer images and manipulate color hues [i.e. green screen] to make a subject transparent.

Cloud Based-Streaming - Streaming and video production interaction that occurs within the cloud, therefore accessible beyond a single user's computer device.

Color Matching - The process of managing color and lighting settings on multiple cameras to match their appearance.

Community Strategy - The strategy of building one's brand and product recognition by building meaningful relationships with an audience, partner, and clientele base.

Content Delivery Network [CDN] - A network of servers that deliver web-based content to an end user.

CPU [Central Processing Unit] – This is the main processor inside of your computer, and it is used to run the operating system and your live streaming software.

DAW - Digital Audio Workstation software is used to produce music. It can also be used to interface with multiple devices and other software using MIDI.

DB9 Cable - A common cable connection for camera joystick serial control.

DHCP [Dynamic Host Configuration Protocol] Router - A router with a network management protocol that dynamically sets IP addresses, so the server can communicate with its sources.

Encoder - A device or software that converts your video sources into an RTMP stream. The RTMP stream can be delivered to CDNs such as Facebook or YouTube.

FOH – Front of House is the part of your church that is open to the public. There is generally a FOH audio mix made to fill this space with the appropriate audio.

GPU – Graphics Processing Unit. This is your graphics card which is used for handling video inside your computer.

H.264 & H.265 - Common formats of video recording, compression, and delivery.

HDMI [High Definition Multimedia Interface] - A cable commonly used for transmitting audio/video.

HEVC [High Efficiency Video Coding] - H.265, is an advanced version of h.264 which promises higher efficiency but lacks the general support of h.264 among most software and hardware solutions available today.

IP [Internet Protocol] Camera/Video - A camera or video source that can send and receive information via a network & internet.

IP Control - The ability to control/connect a camera or device via a network or internet.

ISP – Internet Service Provider. This is the company that you pay monthly for your internet service. They will provide you with your internet connection and router.

Latency - The time it takes between sending a signal and the recipient receiving it.

Live Streaming - The process of sending and receiving audio and or video over the internet.

LAN [Local Area Network] - A network of computers linked together in one location.

MIDI [Musical Instrument Digital Interface] - A way to connect a sound or action to a device. (i.e. a keyboard or controller to trigger an action or sound on a stream

Multicast - Multicast is a method of sending data to multiple computers on your LAN without incurring additional bandwidth for each receiver. Multicast is very different from Unicast which is a data transport method that opens a unique stream of data between each sender and receiver. Multicast allows you to broadcast video from a single camera or live streaming computer to multiple destinations inside your church without adding the bandwidth burden on your network.

Multicorder – Also known as an "IsoCorder" is a feature of streaming software that allows the user to record raw footage from camera feed directly to your hard drive. This feature allows you to record multiple video sources at the same time.

NDI® [Network Device Interface] - Software standard developed by NewTek to enable video-compatible products to communicate, deliver, and receive broadcast quality video in high quality, low latency manner that is frame-accurate and suitable for switching in a live production environment.

NDI® Camera - A camera that allows you to send and receive video over your LAN using NDI technology.

NDI® | HX - NDI High Efficiency, optimizes NDI for limited bandwidth environments.

Network - A digital telecommunications network which allows nodes to share resources. In computer networks, computing devices exchange data with each other using connections between nodes.

Network Switch – A network switch is a networking device that connects multiple devices on a computer network using packet switching to receive, process and forward data to the destination device.

NTSC - Video standard used in North America.

OBS – Open Broadcaster Software is one of the industries most popular live streaming software solutions because it is completely free. OBS is available for Mac, PC, and Linux computers.

PAL - Analog video format commonly used outside of North America.

PCIe- Allows for high bandwidth communication between a device and the computer's motherboard. A PCIe card can installed inside a custom-built computer to provide multiple video inputs (such as HDMI or SDI).

PoE - Power over Ethernet.

PTZ - Pan, tilt, zoom.

RS-232 - Serial camera control transmission.

Router – Your internet router is generally provided to you by your internet service provider. This device may include a firewall, WiFi and/or network switch functionality. This device connects your network to the internet.

RTMP [Real Time Messaging Protocol] – Used for live streaming your video over the public internet.

RTSP [Real Time Streaming Protocol] - Network control protocol for streaming from one point to point. Generally, used for transporting video inside your local area network.

vMix® – vMix is a live streaming software built for Windows computers. It is a professional favorite with high-end features such as low latency capture, NDI support, instant replay, multi-view and much more.

Wirecast® – Wirecast is a live streaming software available for both Mac and PCs with advanced features such as five layers of overlays, lower thirds, virtual sets and much more.

xSplit® – xSplit is a live streaming software with a free and/or low monthly fee paid option. This is a great software available on for Windows computers that combines advanced features and simple to use interface.

About the Author

Paul is the Chief Streaming Officer for StreamGeeks. StreamGeeks is a group of video production experts dedicated to helping organizations discover the power of live streaming.

Every Monday, Paul and his team produce a live show in their downtown West Chester, Pennsylvania studio location. Having produced live shows as amateurs themselves, the StreamGeeks steadily worked their way to a professional level by learning from experience as they went.

Today, they have an impressive following and a tight-knit online community which they serve through consultations and live shows that continue to inspire, motivate, and inform organizations who refuse to settle for mediocrity. The show explores the ever-evolving broadcast and live streaming market while engaging a dedicated live audience.

As a husband and father raising his children in the Lutheran faith, Richards knows a thing or two about the technology inside the church. Richards now specializes in the live streaming media industry leveraging the technology for lead generation. In his book, "Live Streaming is Smart Marketing", Richards reveals his view on lead generation and social media.

Additional Online Courses:

Join over 20,000 other students learning how to leverage the power of live streaming! Take the following courses taught by Paul Richards for free by downloading the course coupon codes available at streamgeeks.us/start.

- **Facebook Live Streaming** - *Beginner*

This course will take your through the Facebook Live basics. It has already been updated twice! This also includes using Facebook Live Reactions!

- **YouTube Live Streaming** - *Beginner*

This course will take you through the YouTube Live basics. It also includes essential branding and tips for marketing.

- **Introduction to OBS (Open Broadcaster Software)**

This course will take your through one of the world's most popular FREE live streaming software solutions. OBS is a great place to start live streaming for free!

- **Introduction to xSplit Software** - *Beginner*

This course takes you through xSplit which has more features that OBS but costs roughly $5/month. Learn how to create amazing live productions and make videos much faster with xSplit!

- **Introduction to vMix** - *Intermediate*

vMix will have you live streaming like the Pros in no time. This Windows based software will amaze even the most advanced video producers!

- **Introduction to Wirecast** - *Intermediate*

Wirecast is the preferred software for so many professional live streamers. Available for Mac or PC this is the ideal software for anyone looking for professional streaming.

- **Introduction to NewTek NDI** - *Intermediate*

NewTek's innovative IP video standard NDI (Network Device Interface) will change the way you think about live video production. Learn how to use this innovative new technology for live streaming and video production system design.

- **Introduction to live streaming course** - *Beginner*

This course includes everything you need to get started designing your show. This course includes a starter pack of course files including: Photoshop, After Effects and free Virtual Sets.

- **Introduction to live streaming** - *Intermediate*

This course focuses on more advanced techniques for optimizing your production workflow and using compression to get the most out of your processor. This course includes files for: Photoshop, After Effects and free Virtual Sets.

- **Live Streaming for Good - Church Streaming Course** - *Intermediate*

This course focuses on live streaming for churches and houses of worship. We tackle some of the big questions about live streaming in a house of worship and dive into the specific challenges of this space.

- **How to Live Streaming A Wedding** - *Beginner*

This is a great course for anyone looking to start live streaming weddings. Originally designed for Wedding Photographers to add a live streaming service to their existing portfolio of offerings. This course is great for beginners

References

- 4 Ridiculously Easy Ways to Generate Revenue with Live Video. (2018, September 24). Retrieved September 20, 2019, from Dacast website: https://www.dacast.com/blog/how-to-make-money-broadcasting-live-video/

- 20 Creative Event Promotion Ideas to Increase Attendance—Eventbrite. (2018, July 20). Retrieved September 19, 2019, from Eventbrite US Blog website: https://www.eventbrite.com/blog/creative-event-promotion-ideas-ds00/

- 20 Event Branding Tips To Run Your Next Event. (2016, February 18). Retrieved September 18, 2019, from Ticketbooth website: https://www.ticketbooth.com.au/ticketing/blog/20-pro-event-branding-tips-running-next-event/

- *31 Best Ways to Sell Tickets for Your Event.* (2019). Retrieved from https://www.eventmanagerblog.com/sell-tickets-events

- admin. (n.d.). Corporate Event Planning – Work Breakdown Structure (WBS) | The Project Diva. Retrieved September 18, 2019, from http://www.theprojectdiva.com/corporate-event-planning—-work-breakdown-structure-wbs/

- Best Live Video Streaming Apps for Mobiles. (2014, December 29). Retrieved September 20, 2019, from Dacast website: https://www.dacast.com/blog/best-live-video-streaming-apps-mobile/

- by. (2019, April 30). How to Choose the Date for an Event: 12 Things to Consider. Retrieved September 17, 2019, from Billetto Blog website: https://billetto.co.uk/blog/how-to-choose-date-for-event/

- Cohen, E. (n.d.). A Beginner-Friendly Guide to Work Breakdown Structures (WBS). Retrieved September 18, 2019, from https://www.workamajig.com/blog/guide-to-work-breakdown-structures-wbs

- Colston, K. (2018, January 25). How To Create Your Event Budget. Retrieved September 17, 2019, from Endless Events website: https://helloendless.com/how-to-create-your-event-budget/

- Evaluating an Event Venue. (2018, March 12). Retrieved September 18, 2019, from Superevent website: https://superevent.com/blog/13-important-things-to-consider-when-choosing-your-event-venue/

- Event Gantt Chart Overview and Example. (2007, May 23). Retrieved September 19, 2019, from Event Manager Blog website: https://www.eventmanagerblog.com/event-gantt-chart

- Event Management: Structure of an event management team. (n.d.). Retrieved September 19, 2019, from http://www.leoisaac.com/evt/top549.htm

- Event Industry by Type. Allied Market Research. Abhishek Roy , Roshan Deshmukh. 2019. Retrieved from https://www.alliedmarketresearch.com/events-industry-market

- How to Create an Event Marketing Plan. (2019, April 11). Retrieved September 19, 2019, from GEVME Blog website: https://www.gevme.com/blog/how-to-create-an-event-marketing-plan/

- How to live stream an event: A step-by-step guide to live streaming events. (2019, April 25). Retrieved September 20, 2019, from Epiphan Video website: https://www.epiphan.com/blog/live-streaming-events/

- How to Market an Event: 50 Event Marketing Tips. (2015, February 19). Retrieved September 19, 2019, from Orbit Media Studios website: https://www.orbitmedia.com/blog/how-to-market-an-event/

- How To Promote An Event: 10 Tips For Promoting Your Event. (n.d.). Retrieved September 19, 2019, from Billetto UK website: https://billetto.co.uk/l/how-to-promote-an-event

- How to Secure Event Sponsorship. (2019, June 25). Retrieved September 17, 2019, from Eventbrite UK website: https://www.eventbrite.co.uk/blog/guide-to-event-sponsorship-ds00/

Paul William Richards

- Hunt, A. (2015, April 14). Licensing and Permissions for Planning a Public Event. Retrieved September 17, 2019, from SMALL BUSINESS CEO website: http://www.smbceo.com/2015/04/14/licensing-and-permissions-for-planning-a-public-event/

- Kaiser, M. (2018, November 16). How to Build "The Dream Team" of Event Planning. Retrieved September 18, 2019, from Endless Events website: https://helloendless.com/how-to-build-a-dream-event-planning-team/

- PayWall. (n.d.). Retrieved September 20, 2019, from https://www.paywall.com/

- Private Live Streaming & Selling Virtual Tickets. (n.d.). Retrieved September 20, 2019, from Udemy website: https://www.udemy.com/course/virtual-tickets/

- Role Up, Roll Out: How to Align Your Teams For the Most Effective Event Strategy. (n.d.). Retrieved September 19, 2019, from https://splashthat.com/blog/event-marketing-plan-team-strategy

- Selling Event Virtual Tickets and Private Live Streams. (2017, October 17). Retrieved September 20, 2019, from StreamGeeks website: https://streamgeeks.us/selling-event-virtual-tickets-private-live-streams/

- Social Media Giving Statistics For Nonprofits. Non-Profit Source, 2019. Retrieved from https://nonprofitssource.com/online-giving-statistics/social-media/

- Spradlin, D. (2012, September 1). Are You Solving the Right Problem? *Harvard Business Review*, (September 2012). Retrieved from https://hbr.org/2012/09/are-you-solving-the-right-problem

- Team, E. (2019, August 3). How to Boost your Ticket Sales with a Virtual Event. Retrieved September 20, 2019, from Online Event registration and Ticket Software—Blog website: https://blog.eventzilla.net/event-planning-tips/how-to-boost-your-ticket-sales-with-a-virtual-event/

- The Experience Economy. Pine, Joseph. Gilmore, James. Harvard Business Review Press. 2020.

- The Ultimate Guide to Event Branding | Eventbrite. (2019, March 21). Retrieved September 18, 2019, from Eventbrite US Blog website: https://www.eventbrite.com/blog/ultimate-guide-to-event-branding-ds00/

- Venue considerations when livestreaming events. (2018, May 28). Retrieved September 20, 2019, from Kiva Solutions website: https://kivasolutions.com/venue-considerations-when-livestreaming-events/

- Video Distribution: Get Access to a Powerful Video CDN. (2018, August 20). Retrieved September 20, 2019, from Dacast website: https://www.dacast.com/blog/live-streaming-cdn/

- Want to Monetize your live stream at your next event? - StreamGeeks. (n.d.). Retrieved September 20, 2019, from https://streamgeeks.us/selling-virtual-event-tickets-nab-ny/

- What is Facebook doing for GivingTuesday? (Facebook, 2019) Retrieved from https://www.facebook.com/help/332488213787105.
- What is a KPI? Definition, Best-Practices, and Examples. (n.d.). Retrieved September 19, 2019, from Klipfolio.com website: https://www.klipfolio.com/resources/articles/what-is-a-key-performance-indicator

- What is a Work Breakdown Structure (WBS)—Workbreakdownstructure.com. (n.d.). Retrieved September 19, 2019, from https://www.workbreakdownstructure.com/

- What is project management? (2017, April 11). Retrieved September 17, 2019, from https://www.apm.org.uk/resources/what-is-project-management/

- Why Do People Attend Events? | Meetings Imagined. (n.d.). Retrieved September 20, 2019, from https://meetingsimagined.com/tips-trends/why-do-people-attend-events

- Work Breakdown Structure (WBS) Examples. (2007, May 18). Retrieved September 19, 2019, from Event Manager Blog website: https://www.eventmanagerblog.com/work-breakdown-structure-wbs-examples/

The Virtual Ticket

Printed in Great Britain
by Amazon

43243333R00078